The
EMOTIONAL
INVESTOR

HOW BIASES INFLUENCE
YOUR INVESTMENT DECISIONS

…And What You Can Do About It

JAY MOORELAND, MS, CFP

The Emotional Investor:
How Biases Influence Your Investment Decisions
…And What You Can Do About It

Jay Mooreland

8362 Tamarack Village

Suite 119-265

Saint Paul, MN 55125

(651) 621-5712

www.theEmotionalinvestor.org

Paperback
Expert

www.PaperbackExpert.com

Disclaimer

While the author has used his best efforts in preparing this book, he makes no representation or warranties with respect to accuracy or completeness of the contents of this book. The advice and strategies contained herein may not be suitable for your situation. You should consult a professional where appropriate. The author shall not be liable for any loss of profit or any other special, incidental, consequential or other damages. The purchaser or reader of this publication assumes responsibility for the use of these materials and information. Adherence to all applicable laws and regulations, both advertising and all other aspects of doing business in the United States or any other jurisdiction, is the sole responsibility of the purchaser of reader.

Table of Contents

Chapter Thirteen

INTRODUCTION

"You never want a serious crisis to go to waste."[1]

—Rahm Emanuel

My Story

The crisis was the financial meltdown of 2008. I didn't expect it, and like many people was not ready for it. But I wasn't just an investor; I was an investment advisor. I was the person people relied on to plan out their financial future and select investments to help them reach their financial goals. Investors that entrusted me with their money had prudent strategies and maintained diversified portfolios. But the crisis was severe, and most asset classes experienced significant losses, even the diversified portfolios.

The experts did not predict the crisis. Just months before the financial market seized up, Federal Reserve Chairman Ben Bernanke told us that we should not be concerned. We were told the collapse of Bear Stearns and other problems were confined to the subprime space. That was not just an understatement; it was wrong.

The crisis was widespread and, for a period, seized up the global financial markets. The markets sold off precipitously. I felt horrible about what happened. I felt misled by Wall Street, by

---

1 Emanuel, Rahm. Interview with *Wall Street Journal*. Retrieved August 4, 2015 at https://www.youtube.com/watch?v=1yeA_kHHLow

the Fed and by all the "experts." I was emotionally charged with regret; my clients were relying on me to help them reach their goals, and I felt that I had let them down. How I wished I could have seen it coming.

As I sorted through the events, I realized I could do nothing about the past, so I had to prepare for the future. I did not want to get caught off guard like this again because my clients trusted me with their hard-earned money. I realized that Wall Street was not going to help. The truth is that Wall Street is positively biased. Seldom, if ever, do you find a major investment firm predicting bad times. I realized that negative forecasts from the Fed or major financial institutions could *cause* the market to go down. A negative forecast could be a self-fulfilling prophecy.

The bottom line is that market experts cannot be truly unbiased. Yet I could. So I decided to return to school. I wanted to learn more about economics. I wanted to learn how these economists make their predictions and what models they use so I could form an *unbiased* opinion.

But at school I didn't learn what I expected to learn, and what I learned changed everything about the way I approach investing. I learned why economic forecasts are often wrong. It's because of assumptions, faulty assumptions.

Assumptions

There is nothing inherently wrong with making assumptions. We make them in everyday life. We make assumptions when we lack sufficient data; they are a necessary part of life. But sometimes in economics the assumptions are dead wrong.

One of the most erroneous assumptions is the notion that investors act rationally. To a layperson, rationality may be defined as having common sense and levelheaded thinking. Yet in the investment realm, a rational individual is one who doesn't make any mistakes and is not influenced by emotions.

Harry Markowitz, the creator of the Modern Portfolio Theory (MPT), assumed that the investor is rational. Many Wall Street tools and methodologies make that same assumption. But Mr. Markowitz understood his own fallacy. Even after he proposed his theory based on rationality, he admitted: "The Rational Man, like the unicorn, does not exist."[2]

That became a key principle as I finished my graduate work and developed new thinking about investing. I directed a significant percentage of research for my thesis on what are referred to as "behavioral biases," "behavioral tendencies," or "preferences" that influence our decisions. And most of these influences are subconscious, meaning we are not aware of their influence.

Behavioral Economics

Behavioral economics, rather than assuming or saying how we should act, is all about questioning our intuition and the thoughts and emotions that go into the decision-making process. Traditional finance, which is what most investment tools are based on, is about how people *should* behave; behavioral economics is about how people *actually* behave. Economist Richard Thaler noted that traditional "economic theory presumes that self-control problems do not exist."[3] And yet they do.

---

2 Markowitz, Harry. *Portfolio Selection: Efficient Diversification of Investments.* ©1959. John Wiley & Sons. New York. Page 206.

3 Thaler, Richard H. *Misbehaving: The Making of Behavioral Economics.* ©2015. W.W. Norton & Company. New York. Page 86.

Most tools that financial professionals use today do not account for the "human element." A common tool used by Wall Street professionals is called an optimizer. An optimizer is an algorithm that provides the best or optimal response to a question. It requires certain inputs before it can produce a response. And optimizers assume investors behave rationally (no mistakes or emotions) at all times.

The MPT introduced an investment optimizer known as the Mean-Variance Optimizer. One of the questions it answers is: What allocation of securities will maximize my return for a given level of risk? After providing the necessary inputs of expected future return, variance, and covariance, the optimizer provides the answer: "This is the optimal allocation for you." And it would be optimal, if only we were void of emotion and never made mistakes.

When we hear the word "optimal," our brain automatically drops its skepticism and says: "I'm going to follow that." If something is optimal, that means it's the best. We want to have it. The problem is that optimizers are built for the rational being, not the human being.

I'm more of a realist than I am a theorist. Behavioral economics, also known as behavioral finance, highlights the significance of living in reality. It's important to recognize who you are today and to make decisions about becoming better down the road.

Focus on What You Can Control

We want to be sure that we focus on those things we can control. Many investors spend the majority of their time considering factors that are beyond their control. We constantly wonder what the market is going to do, what sectors will outperform, where interest rates are heading, and what policy changes government may make.

Yet we spend very little time thinking about issues over which we have complete control—things like our investment process and plan, and how we are going to react to future market events.

Jason Zweig, a columnist for *The Wall Street Journal* and author, wrote this profoundly simple truth: "Investing intelligently is about controlling the controllable."[4]

That's what this book is all about: learning to subdue emotional influences and make more deliberate and thoughtful financial decisions. Emotional investing may *feel* good, but thoughtful investing *is* good.

The Cost of Emotional Investing

We all know the investment adage is "buy low, sell high." But it is emotionally easier to buy high and sell low.

Emotional investing often results in making hasty decisions based on short-term outcomes. Many times these decisions end up being very costly mistakes—either by losing money or by being out of the market when it is soaring.

A firm by the name of DALBAR, Inc. does extensive analysis on the cost of investor behavior. The firm's report, Quantitative Analysis of Investor Behavior, has found that investors significantly underperform their benchmark index, as evidenced by the charts below.[5]

---

4 Graham, Benjamin. *The Intelligent Investor–Revised Edition.* ©2003. HarperCollins. New York. Page 219.

5 Source: "Quantitative Analysis of Investor Behavior, 2015," DALBAR, Inc.

Both stock and bond investors, on average, significantly underperformed their respective benchmark in 2014.

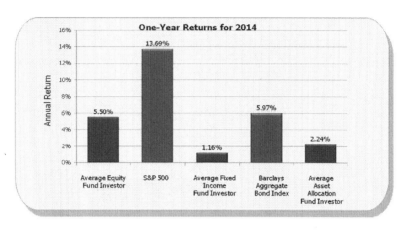

And they have also underperformed over longer periods of time.

		Investor Returns[1]					Barclays
	Equity Funds	Asset Allocation Funds	Fixed Income Funds	Composite Fund Investor	Inflation	S&P 500	Aggregate Bond Index
30 Year	3.79	1.76	0.72	2.47	2.70	11.06	7.36
20 Year	5.19	2.47	0.80	3.34	2.28	9.85	6.20
10 Year	5.26	2.25	0.69	3.51	2.13	7.67	4.71
5 Year	10.19	5.09	1.21	6.84	1.69	15.45	4.45
3 Year	14.82	7.15	0.72	9.57	1.34	20.41	2.66
12 Months	5.50	2.24	1.16	3.98	0.75	13.69	5.97

1. Returns are for the period ending December 31, 2014. *Average equity investor, average bond investor and average asset allocation investor performance results are calculated using data supplied by the Investment Company Institute. Investor returns are represented by the change in total mutual fund assets after excluding sales, redemptions and exchanges. This method of calculation captures realized and unrealized capital gains, dividends, interest, trading costs, sales charges, fees, expenses and any other costs. After calculating investor returns in dollar terms, two percentages are calculated for the period examined: Total investor return rate and annualized investor return rate. Total return rate is determined by calculating the investor return dollars as a percentage of the net of the sales, redemptions and exchanges for each period.*

DALBAR, Inc. further goes on to report that the underperformance is due to the *timing* of purchases and sales of securities. This is because investors often buy securities after they go up and sell them after they have experienced a loss. It is a negative detractor to performance. Of course, these are just averages. Some investment decisions we make are really good and add to our overall return. But many decisions, especially those made when our emotions are high, can eradicate past gains and reduce the likelihood of reaching our financial goals.

As we adjust our portfolio based upon market conditions and expectations in order to improve our overall return, we actually accomplish the exact opposite. The evidence proves it. The more often we tinker with our portfolios, the worse we tend to do.

Benjamin Graham, the father of value investing and mentor of Warren Buffett, has said: "The investor's chief problem—and even his own worst enemy—is likely to be himself."[6]

I couldn't agree more, but we're about to change that.

My Notes

_____

_____

_____

_____

_____

_____

6 Graham, Benjamin. *The Intelligent Investor–Revised Edition.* ©2003. HarperCollins. New York. Page 8.

SECTION 1

Why We Do
What We Do

Chapter One

Thinking and Feeling

There is a time to lead with thought and a time to lead with feeling. Knowing which one to lead with is the challenge.

The brain is a very complex organ. It represents only 2 percent of our body weight, yet burns 20 percent of our body's energy. Daniel Kahneman, one of the fathers of behavioral finance, does an excellent job presenting this complex organ in a simple fashion. His book titled *Thinking, Fast and Slow* describes the brain as being comprised of two systems, System 1 and System 2.

System 1 is the first responder. This is where we go first to answer questions or solve problems. It operates automatically, subconsciously, with little to no effort. It is our default responder. To make judgments, it relies upon intuition, stereotypes, memories and heuristics (mental shortcuts). It also tends to identify causal connections between events, even when there is none. The primary role of System 1 is to act based on impressions and feelings.

These feelings include feelings of pleasure and pain; however, they are not felt equally. When it comes to investing, financial loss (pain) causes a more intense feeling than does an equal size gain (pleasure). In fact, research has demonstrated that the pain of loss is at least twice as intense as the pleasure from an equal size gain.

System 1 is also known as the reflexive system. Think about a knee-jerk reaction. Truly, it's a reflex. You receive some sort of input—your doctor whacks your knee with a mallet—and it immediately spits out an output: the leg kicks involuntarily. You don't have to think about it. In fact, even if you try to keep your leg still, the reflexive impulse will win; the leg will still pop up when hit with the mallet.

Our brain works in a similar fashion. Conscious attention is not required to generate a response. We don't need to think about it. When stimulus comes, System 1 responds. This automatic, intuitive, and reflexive system is the default responder in life. It handles most of our questions and problems in life—including when we make financial decisions.

System 2 is our thinking brain. This is where we employ logic, consider the future, and exercise self-control—what are often referred to as executive or higher-order functions. The ability to think, plan, and control our behavior is what sets humans apart from other species that have a brain.

The challenge is that System 2 requires concentration and effort. We must consciously engage this part of the brain; it is not a default or automatic response. We can engage it by asking reflective questions such as, "How could I be wrong?" or "What is the evidence of this?" System 2 requires not only brainpower to reflect and ask deeper questions, but also sufficient time to analyze the situation and to respond.

System 2 can only entertain one conscious thought or problem at a time. If System 2 is preoccupied trying to solve a problem, System 1 will automatically respond to any additional stimuli. When it comes to System 2, there is no such thing as multitasking, just switching quickly between tasks. So it's very important that when we're making a financial decision—whether it's budgeting, making a large purchase, or investing—that our mind is clear of distractions. We need to engage System 2.

Engaging System 2 requires effort and takes energy. The brain, like the body, prefers less effort to more. When we receive a stimulus and need to solve a problem or make a decision, we tend to go with the reflexive system. With System 1, the answer is immediate and effortless—it doesn't consume energy. System 2, on the other hand, drains our energy…quickly. For that reason, the brain's default response is System 1.

There is a biological necessity that System 1 is our default response. Our mind handles roughly 11 million bits of information *per second.*[7] The conscious mind is estimated to handle only 50 bits per second. If we were to try to handle all incoming information using System 2, we would have a complete meltdown. Biologically, we are made so that we can function in everyday life.

But some matters, such as financial decisions, need thought—so we must consciously engage that function of our brain. We need to make a conscious effort to reduce emotional impulses and distractions so that we can give System 2 the time to thoughtfully consider the options at hand.

---

7 Mlodinow, Leonard. *Subliminal: How Your Unconscious Mind Rules Your Behavior.* ©2012. Pantheon Books. New York.

The Physiology of the Brain.

Two parts of our brain that influence our decisions are the limbic system and the prefrontal cortex. The limbic system, also referred to as the "lizard brain," is where our most basic functions and our natural instincts occur. The primary function of the limbic system is to ensure our survival.

The amygdala is located in the limbic system, which is representative of Kahneman's System 1. The amygdala responds to emotions and threatening situations. When it is activated, the message sent throughout the body is "Get to Safety." It's a neurological response that is basically fight or flight. If you are crossing a street, and you see a car about to hit you, the amygdala springs into action. Within a split second, you will be jumping out of the way before you consciously realize what is happening.

The amygdala is about action. It is the gas pedal of our brain that influences us to do something, and to do it now. When the amygdala is activated, the time for thinking is gone. In fact, one of the features of the amygdala is to hijack the thinking part of our brain (System 2). Have you ever tried to reason with an emotional individual and out of frustration yelled, "You aren't even thinking!"? That is actually a correct statement because he is not thinking. The amygdala has shut down that capability. Biologically, this makes sense. If you were in a dangerous situation that required an immediate response, it would not be wise to think or analyze the situation.

The amygdala is crucial for our survival, but the same response can cause us much anguish when it comes to investing. Neuroscientists have found through functional MRI (fMRI) that when people are experiencing financial loss, their amygdala may activate. And the message the amygdala sends? Get to safety. A

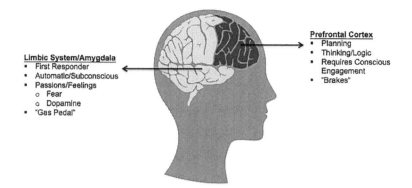

Limbic System/Amygdala
- First Responder
- Automatic/Subconscious
- Passions/Feelings
  - Fear
  - Dopamine
- "Gas Pedal"

Prefrontal Cortex
- Planning
- Thinking/Logic
- Requires Conscious Engagement
- "Brakes"

trusted advisor or friend may encourage us to stay the course and focus on the long term. But the amygdala cares about the now, not the future. The amygdala is basically telling us there may not be a tomorrow. The amygdala causes us to overestimate the risk because we don't see how the situation could ever improve…it's only going to get worse.

It *feels* good to follow the promptings of the amygdala. Fighting the amygdala is like withstanding the urge to scratch a mosquito bite—it makes us very uncomfortable and goes against our greatest desire. Giving in to the amygdala is like scratching the bite—it provides temporary relief but often makes things worse. And when it comes to investing, that can be a very costly and only temporary reprieve.

Neuroscientists have also found through fMRI that dopamine can be released in the brains of people who are experiencing or simply imagining a financial gain. In fact, neuroscientists said that the brain images of those experiencing financial gains were indistinguishable from someone high on drugs.[8]

---

8 Zweig, Jason. *Your Money & Your Brain.* ©2007. Simon & Schuster. New York.

Dopamine is a neurotransmitter that produces feelings of pleasure, optimism, and confidence. The confidence and optimism from dopamine may cause investors to underestimate risk simply because they don't see the downside... they don't see how they can be wrong. And if you are sure of something, you don't want to buy just a little bit of it, you want to buy a lot of it. So dopamine can result in investors creating portfolios that contain more risk than they are able to handle.

While investors know they should buy low and sell high, the amygdala and dopamine explain why many investors do the exact opposite. It is easier to buy high and sell low; it *feels* better to buy high and sell low. Allowing emotions to influence investment decisions may provide temporary relief, but it often comes at a long-term cost.

The Prefrontal Cortex

The prefrontal cortex controls our executive functions such as planning, logic, problem solving, and concentration. It's also our inhibitor. The amygdala is the gas pedal (act now), and the prefrontal cortex is our brake (slow down and reflect). This is System 2. To benefit from System 2, we must consciously engage it. We need to put forth the effort and allow time to consider the options, weigh the choices, and settle on the best decision.

The amygdala is only interested in providing comfort for the immediate time period, irrespective of any long-term consequence. The prefrontal cortex, because of its ability to plan and project long-term outcomes, is essential to use when it comes to making financial decisions.

Amygdala: "Act now."

Prefrontal cortex: "Not so fast."

The way our brains are hardwired is extremely efficient and effective at living life. But when it comes to investing, it's almost like we are hardwired to be bad investors. The key is to override our natural instincts by engaging the thinking part of our brain.

Engaging the Thinking Brain

The first step to engaging the thinking brain is to delay our response. Then we need to distract ourselves from the issue at hand. Remember that when emotions are high and danger is perceived, the amygdala is in control and has likely hijacked (temporarily) the prefrontal cortex. We need to get away so the impulse doesn't influence us to make a hasty decision. We want to scratch the mosquito bite—we know we will feel better. Yet, it is better to put ice on it. Cooling off the bite will reduce the itch; in the same way, giving yourself time to cool off will reduce your likelihood of making a poor decision. Get out and do something completely different. Getting out of a room only to think about it more is not the answer. We need to distract ourselves. Whether by cutting the grass or starting an unrelated project, we must delay and distract.

And consider this: A delay is an action. So it is not as if you aren't doing anything by delaying. Your action is a delay. You are consciously *choosing* to delay.

Step two is to ask yourself the right questions during the delay. You need to make sure you're thinking about the situation logically, not emotionally. Here are a few suggestions that you may want to consider when experiencing financial losses and want to "get to safety":

- In prior market crashes, such as Black Monday in 1987 and the 2008 financial crisis, how did the markets perform seven years later?

Write your answer below.

Black Monday:_____   Financial Crisis:_____

- Is the current crisis likely to be worse than those? Yes/No
- Is my time horizon greater than seven years? Yes/No

If an investor has a long-term time horizon (defined as seven years in this case), history has shown it has paid handsomely to hang in there. Seven years after Black Monday, the market not only recouped its losses, it increased an *additional* 71 percent. After the financial crisis of 2008, the market not only recovered all of its losses but also went up an *additional* 80 percent.[9]

So within seven years of both crises, the markets not only recouped all the losses but also gained … significantly. But those investors who were compelled to sell during the fearful times failed to participate in the gains.

While hanging in there during significant short-term losses is quite a feat, it isn't the most optimal solution. What about buying low? Now you are in the position to ask yourself the better question, "How can I take advantage of these low prices for my long-term gain?"

That's what gets the planning brain going because now you're thinking forward. Focus less on your current feelings and on what caused yesterday's drop, and focus more on how you can benefit from others' mistakes.

---

9   Both examples use SPY and assume reinvestment of dividends. Portfolio returns for Black Monday example from Oct 5, 1987 to Oct 5, 1994. Portfolio returns for Financial Crisis example from June 2, 2008 to June 1, 2015.

Key Takeaways

① The brain can be simplified into two main functions: reflexive (hasty decisions) and reflective (thoughtful decisions).

② Our reflexive brain (System 1) is our default response system. It's responses are immediate, automatic and effortless.

③ The reflective brain (System 2) requires conscious engagement, effort and discipline.

④ Emotional investing may provide temporary satisfaction and feel good, but thoughtful investing is good.

My Notes

Chapter Two

Volatile Market, Volatile Behavior

Volatility doesn't cause losses; it's our reaction to volatility that causes losses.

The financial markets have always been volatile. From their inception, we have seen price swings on a daily basis. At times, the volatility is muted; at other times it has been quite extreme. The Great Depression, Black Monday, Technology Bubble Burst, and the recent Financial Crisis all experienced significant volatility and severe losses.

Most investors are uncomfortable with volatility. When volatility increases it is often accompanied by negative news and market losses–causing fear and sometimes panic. Volatility is a major contributor to activating the amygdala. And once the amygdala activates, the message is, "Get to safety! Sell!"

It is more constructive, and in our economic interest, to view volatility as an opportunity. Today volatility may be our foe, but we can make it our friend. Volatility creates opportunities for long-term investors to acquire assets at a discount. Black Friday is a great shopping day because of the sales. It is funny how we look forward to Black Friday (and every retail sale), but we fear when financial assets go on sale. Volatility provides the "seasonal sale" for financial assets.

When we witness the market's apparent random movements, up one day, down the next day, we tend to get uncomfortable; we may need to reach for the bottle of Pepto Bismol. Emotionally, we would prefer it if the markets just moved higher—a little bit every day would be nice. But financially, we can greatly improve our returns by taking advantage of the volatility and "seasonal sales."

The markets tend to trend over time. Bull markets are when the market is trending higher–and just about everyone is making money. Bear markets are when the market is trending lower–and we are becoming poorer each day. There are other times when there is no discernible trend; up one day, down the next. Up one month, down the next month. You see a nice period of gains, only to find the gains vanish (and then some) over the next period. Watching this stuff can make you seasick.

But that's the way the market always has been. If you aren't comfortable with the degree of volatility, you have two options:

1. Don't invest—but you may not be able to reach your financial goals.

2. Quit watching the market.

If I don't like the feeling of punching myself in the face, you would tell me, "Don't punch yourself in the face." If volatility makes you anxious, if it makes you jittery, if you find that it leads you to make bad investment decisions, then don't look. Just because the market information is easily available does not mean the information is valuable or beneficial to you. Statistical inference says that increased information will increase your knowledge, but that is not always true in real life. In fact, the daily news, the daily volatility, the instant quotation—are often detrimental to our financial well-being.

You can't control the volatility of the market, but you have complete control over how much volatility you experience. Volatility is largely subjective.

Take Joe and Jane. They both purchase ACME Fund at $70 a share. Joe tracks the security movement every day, and Jane doesn't. After a year, each sells the security for $77, so each realized a 10 percent gain. But since Joe tracked the market daily, he experienced a significant amount of volatility. He saw it go up. Perhaps it went well over $80, and he saw it drop to $60. And witnessed every price movement in between.

Jane never once looked at the price of the fund. She bought it at $70 and sold it for $77. Her profit was identical to Joe's. But she earned her return without the drama and anxiety that Joe experienced.

The markets will do what they do, whether you watch or not. The truth of the matter is, however, that the more you watch, the more the volatility will tempt you to make financial decisions based upon short-term outcomes.

Consider the two investment options on the following page. Which investment would you prefer? Why?

Investment A:

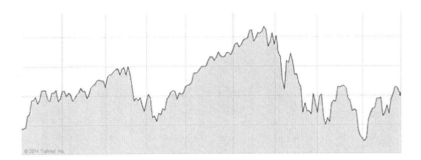

Investment B:

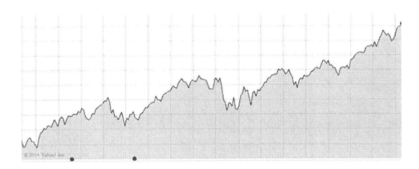

Investment A is a volatile investment that goes up and down without any defined trend. You start and end with about the same amount of money. Investment B has a clear upward trend. So what is the difference between Investment A and B? Not much. They are the same investment: the S&P 500. Investment A is simply a nine-month period of time *within* Investment B.

The dots at the bottom of the chart of Investment B represent the nine-month period of Investment A. This illustrates that even great long-term investments (B) can look downright awful over shorter periods of time (A). And had you been influenced to sell because the security was volatile and appeared to go nowhere, you would have missed out on significant long-term gains.

You can't control the volatility of the markets. But if you want to reduce the amount of volatility you personally experience, it is best to stop looking, or at the very least to evaluate performance over longer intervals of time.

The Value of Volatility

There is some good in volatility. Volatility reminds us that there is risk in the markets. While we would all *feel* better about the markets moving higher each day, periods of low volatility can give us a false sense of security. With this false perception that risk is low, we may be tempted to take on more risks, and not realize it until we end up losing more than we were prepared to lose. Volatility can help keep our risk in check.

Volatility also provides lower prices. We like that. We like lower prices at the clothing store. We like lower prices at the grocery store. The only place we don't like lower prices is in the financial markets. We need to change that thinking. If you like a company at $50 a share, you should probably love it at $40. The economy is cyclical; companies do well over some period of time, and they do poorly at other periods of time. If you are a long-term investor, and you believe that a company (or the market as a whole) is going to grow over time, you ought to get excited about lower prices. It allows you to purchase financial assets for less money. It's the "sale of the season" for stocks.

Volatility in the markets creates stress. Most of the time we view stress as a negative force. But stress, in reasonable amounts, is actually beneficial and necessary. If you are at the gym trying to strengthen a muscle, you lift weights. That weight acts as a stress to the muscle, ultimately making it stronger. If a muscle were to never be stressed, it would be in a state of atrophy. This also applies to our psyche. With occasional stress, we learn how to deal with it, and it makes our personality and spirit stronger. Many people, having lived through a very stressful tragedy, will look back and view that stress as something that made them the person they are today. They dealt with the situation and made the most of it. Without stresses, it is very hard to progress in life.

Without volatility, we may not be able to progress as investors. It doesn't take much to invest in an FDIC-insured CD (which exhibits zero volatility). The past years of artificially suppressed volatility give the perception that there is no risk out there. I am not advocating for a significant degree of volatility; that would not be good. I do believe that more frequent, low-magnitude volatility can be very beneficial for the investor. Frequent volatility will discourage investors from speculating on short-term outcomes, and they will need to adapt to a longer-term view of things—which is what investors should do in the first place. Volatility doesn't cause losses; it's investors' reaction to volatility that causes losses. In a recent LinkedIn post, Dr. Daniel Crosby said, "It is simply hard to overstate the wealth-destroying impact of volatility-borne irrationality."[10] If we become accustomed to the presence of volatility, we will be less likely to act irrationally when it happens in the future, thus making us better investors.

Key Takeaways

① Volatility is subjective. By evaluating our performance less frequently, we experience less volatility.

② Volatility can be our friend. Volatility provides attractive prices for long-term investors.

③ Volatility reminds us that there are risks, and helps us focus more on the long-term potential.

My Notes

_____

_____

_____

_____

10   Crosby, Daniel, "The Behavioral Benefits of Diversification." Published on Linkedin March 2, 2015

SECTION 2

Obtaining the
Correct Perspective

Chapter Three

Myopic Thinking

"If owning stocks is a long-term project for you, following their changes constantly is … the worst possible thing you can do."[11]

—Daniel Kahneman

Myopia, or nearsightedness, is a common vision condition. Most of us are familiar with the term and know someone who cannot see distant objects clearly without corrective lenses or eye surgery. Few people have heard of financial myopia, yet it is just as prevalent as nearsightedness, if not more. Financial myopia is less nearsightedness and more shortsightedness. It's not that investors lack the ability to view things at a distance; instead, they *choose* to focus on short-term outcomes. We are all free to choose, but this choice can be costly.

Our physiological desire for immediate feedback (instant gratification) plays a significant role in our life and influences financial myopia. The fresh-baked chocolate chip cookies, the extra hour of sleep in the morning, the car you can drive away in today

---

11 Zweig, Jason. *Your Money & Your Brain.* ©2007. Simon & Schuster. New York. Page 83.

with no money down. These are all things that provide immediate pleasure to our physiological selves while delaying their costs. The incentive is strong and many times we'll receive a small dose of dopamine, giving us a pleasurable feeling we desire. While we are unlikely to say, "Wow, I just got a hit of dopamine," our mood may improve and we may experience temporary pleasure. Otherwise, we wouldn't be influenced to engage in the activity. We overvalue the reward we receive today while undervaluing the price we will pay in the future. Economists refer to this as having a high discount rate.

In a similar fashion, we are physiologically encouraged to evaluate our financial situation in the short term. The reward is a bit different. Instead of satisfying our sweet tooth, desire for more sleep, or the thrill that comes from buying a new car, what investors really want—according to psychologist Dr. Daniel Crosby—is simplicity, safety, and surety. In the case of financial myopia, investors really want surety. We want to know we are doing the right thing and will reach our end goals.

The illusion of control also influences financial myopia—the illusion that investors can use current news and market outcomes to determine what changes to make so they can increase the certainty of reaching their goals. The problem is many studies show this behavior results in achieving lower returns, therefore, less surety. (See DALBAR Inc. findings on page 14).

The financial media adds fuel to the fire. The constant discussion about the big news story of the day, the sense of urgency they portray, the continuous intraday quotations of market indices, and the experts predicting what the market will do in the near future all influence investors to focus on short-term outcomes.

MW Market Watch

Get ready for a real lousy month in the stock market

The financial media is there to get you to tune in, not to help you reach your goals. Viewer beware. Our physiology and the financial media influence financial myopia, regardless of our stated time horizon.

Here are some interesting statistics about investing:

- A portfolio with an expected return of 15 percent and volatility of 10 percent has a 93 percent probability of positive returns in any one year. Yet that same portfolio has a probability of being positive in a given month of only 67 percent.[12] *In other words, a good long-term portfolio can be highly volatile and appear unattractive in the short term.*

- A good process may produce bad results in the short term. A bad process may produce good results in the short term. It is only over time that a good process will demonstrate

---

12 Taleb, Nassim Nicholas. *Fooled By Randomness.* ©2004. Random House. New York.

good outcomes and vice versa.[13] *Short-term outcomes are not evidence of whether your investment strategy is good or not.*

- Over the past 20 years, six of the 10 best days for the S&P 500 occurred within two weeks of the 10 worst days.[14] *Allowing short-term outcomes to influence your investment strategy can be very costly.*

True investors evaluate their portfolios over long periods of time. Speculators are interested in short-term results. However, many long-term investors, unbeknownst to themselves, actually act like speculators. The way that you can tell whether you are acting more like a speculator than an investor is to ask yourself the question: "Am I more interested in the short-term stock price movement than I am in the value of the underlying company?"

If you are, you are speculating. Stock price movement in the short-term is often detached from the underlying value of the company and is heavily influenced by the mood of investors and traders. We have seen many examples of this, such as the Ebola scare in October 2014 and the Greece/Euro concern during the summer of 2015. Stock prices went down and rebounded quickly while the intrinsic value of the underlying companies remained unchanged.

If you make investment decisions based upon short-term stock-price movements, you are speculating because you are doing it based upon something that has little (if anything) to do with the underlying value of the company.

---

13 Mauboussin, Michael J. *The Success Equation: Untangling Skill and Luck in Business Sports and Investing.* ©2012. Harvard Review Business Press. Boston.

14 J.P. Morgan. 2015 Guide to Retirement.

"Over a short time increment, one observes the variability of the portfolio, not the returns."[15]

—Nassim Taleb

Sometimes, investing based upon short-term results can appear to be the right thing to do. Oftentimes, when people make a decision, they want instant feedback that the decision was a good one.

If the market is losing money, and I panic and sell, I'll look at the market the next day and the odds are I will see it go even lower (few people actually sell the day the market hits bottom). I'll breathe a big sigh of relief and think: "Whew, I did the right thing." This same desire for instant feedback also happens when we buy high.

The problem is that what appears right in the short term is often wrong in the long term. Consider the example comparing the results of an investor who focused on those things she could control (utilizing an investment plan) to another that speculated on future returns with no set strategy.

The following charts illustrate the performance of two identical investors beginning in June 2007 with a portfolio of 70 percent stocks and 30 percent bonds. Jane had a process that specified a rebalancing strategy. Joe had no such plan but very good intentions. Joe always planned to buy low and sell high but

---

15   Taleb, Nassim Nicholas. *Fooled by Randomness.* ©2004. Random House, New York. Page 67.

was influenced by portfolio losses and pessimistic forecasts to sell stocks at the end of October 2008.[16]

Over the short term, it appears that Joe was wise in selling stocks and moving all assets to bonds as evidenced by his outperformance relative to Jane.

March 9, 2009

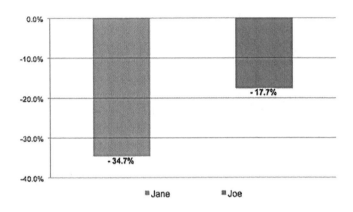

At the end of March, Joe will see his losses, but realize they would have been a lot worse had he remained invested. He may say to himself, "I did the right thing." This confirms to him that investing on emotions/instinct was a good thing. But this is dangerous, because what looks to be right in the short term is not an indication of whether it was a wise decision in the long term.

---

16 Jane had a strategy of rebalancing every year if the allocation deviated 5 percent or more from the target. In this scenario, she rebalanced on the last business day of May in 2008, 2009, 2011, and 2014. Joe is assumed to have sold all stocks on October 31, 2008, and invested all into bonds. Performance includes reinvestment of dividends. SPY represented stocks and AGG represented bonds.

We take this example out to 2015, and the patience and diligence Jane demonstrated with her investment process paid off handsomely.

May 31, 2015

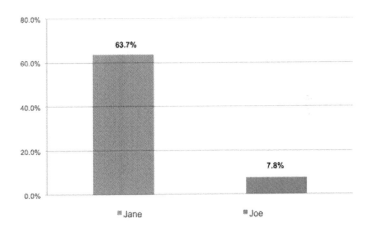

Overcoming Financial Myopia

Financial myopia entails both psychological and financial cost. The constant evaluation of short-term market performance can cause unnecessary anxiety, distract us from more productive activities, and cause us to neglect personal responsibilities. It can cause an investor who has a deliberate, thoughtful investment plan to throw it out because it fails to yield desirable results right away. In addition, financial myopia is a significant drag on investment performance. While financial myopia may appease your short-term emotions and desires, it does so at a significant long-term cost.

Strategic procrastination should be a part of every investment plan.

We want and need instant feedback. Let us not deny our biological desires, but rather change our focus. Instead of focusing on short-term returns as a feedback, it would be more productive to create a customized investment plan and stick to it—whether the sky is falling or the prices are soaring. Following the crowd is easy. Sticking with a winning strategy, especially during times of temporary losses, is hard.

That is your instant feedback. That is what makes you a great investor. You do not allow your emotions to rule. You choose to delay and distract rather than make hasty decisions. You are able to stick to a plan even when the market forces are creating fear and causing everyone else to jump ship.

Key Takeaways

① Deliberately avoid short-term market and economic outcomes.

② Great long-term investments can perform terribly over short periods of time.

③ Create a customized investment plan.

④ Maintain discipline to stick with your plan through thick and thin.

My Notes

Chapter Four

The Illusion of Certainty

"Prediction is very difficult, especially about the future."[17]

———Niels Bohr

Our brain hates uncertainty. Absolutely detests it. Has there been a time when you didn't know the answer or outcome to something and thought: "I don't care if the news is good or bad, just tell me"? The worst is not knowing. This is because the brain finds an immense amount of pleasure in planning and order.

The executive function of the brain is a planning machine. We like to plan. We plan our vacations. We plan what we're going to do tomorrow. We plan what we're going to buy at the grocery store. The planning allows us to be efficient and productive. If you have uncertainty, if you don't know what's going to happen, you can't plan effectively. Even if the news is bad, the brain says, "Okay, it's bad news. But at least I know, and I can figure out the best steps going forward."

17　BrainyQuote.com, Xplore Inc. Retrieved July 28, 2015, at http://www. brainyquote.com/quotes/quotes/n/nielsbohr130288.html

Recently, I was speaking with a friend of the family. This young woman had just broken up with her boyfriend. I went to talk to her, to help her sort through things. Her boyfriend basically asked her to go to her mom's house and give him a few days to think about things. She had been calling him asking: "Just tell me. Are we breaking up, or is this a temporary separation? Because if we're just going to break up, I'll come and get my stuff right now."

Rather than endure the uncertainty, she was actually willing to say, "Let's just break up." She was willing to split up to take the uncertainty out of it. The uncertainty was killing her.

When an analyst confidently predicts what the market or interest rates are going to do, we are subconsciously influenced to believe it because that forecast provides a *false* sense of certainty. And if the analyst is deemed an "expert," we are even more likely to believe. Research shows that when a person is introduced to us as an expert, our brain switches off our natural skepticism. We are inclined to take it as truth.[18]

Here's the problem. The experts are not good at forecasting future outcomes. Numerous studies demonstrate their predictive abilities are no better than random guessing.

- Philip Tetlock, a professor of psychology, reviewed 28,000 prior predictions and forecasts by experts (both financial and non-financial) and found that "experts' predictions barely beat random guesses—the statistical equivalent of a dart-throwing chimp … Ironically, the more famous the

18 Engelmann, JB, Capra, CM, Noussair, C. & Berns GS. 2009. "Expert Financial Advice Neurobiologically 'Offloads' Financial Decision-Making Under Risk" PLoS ONE 4(3): 4857.doi:10.1371/journal.pone.0004957).

expert, the less accurate his or her predictions tended to be."[19]

- In 2014, Goldman Sachs conducted a significant study to predict who would win the World Cup. As part of the study, the firm's analysts researched more than 14,000 prior soccer matches and produced a 67-page report that included their quantitative analysis as well as their predictions. According to an analysis by the *Wall Street Journal*, their predictions were as accurate as random guessing.[20] All that effort and time. Yet the analyses were no better than random guesses. As with all forecasts, Goldman Sachs' experts based their predictions on assumptions, such as that none of the players would be injured. Of course, players got hurt. A couple of key players were hurt, and that may have changed the outcome.

This is the problem with predictions. Oftentimes forecasters assume that nothing unexpected will happen … after all, how can you predict an unexpected event? Yet life is all about unexpected occurrences. When life inevitably throws us a curveball, the outcome is often different than the prediction.

Market and economic forecasts are no different. As you will see below, experts have a history of mis-predicting interest rates, stock prices and GDP. With the history of "misses," we should be careful about how much weight we put behind any forecast.

---

19 Schurenberg, Eric. "Why the Experts Missed the Crash," *Money Magazine*, March 2009.

20 The *Wall Street Journal*. July 10, 2014. "Goldman Sachs's World Cup Predictions Model: Successful?"

Market/Economic Forecasts

- At the end of 2013, *The Wall Street Journal* economist survey showed that 48 of 49 economists predicted the 10-year Treasury interest rate would be higher in 2014 (consensus 3.5 percent) than the current rate of 2.9 percent. In reality, it ended the year at 2.2 percent. Only one of the economists got the direction right.[21]

- CXO Advisory looked at 6,000 market predictions by financial experts (analysts, strategists, economists) and found an overall accuracy rate of 47 percent.[22]

- From 1958 to 2010, actual GDP figures fell outside the 90 percent confidence range of economists' predictions roughly half of the time.[23]

- In July 2008, just a few months before the financial markets seized up, Fed Chairman Ben Bernanke said: "The GSE's (Government-Sponsored Enterprises) are adequately capitalized. They are in no danger of failing."[24] Two months later, they did fail, and the economy entered its worst crisis since the Great Depression. So you have the Fed, with access to all information public and private, just two months before the economy collapsed, saying that there was no danger of failing.

21 The *Wall Street Journal*. December 31, 2014. The Intelligent Investor.

22 Guru Grades, CXO Advisory. Retrieved on August 4, 2015, at http://www.cxoadvisory.com/gurus/

23 Clements, Michael P. "An Evaluation of the Survey of Professional Forecasts Probability Distribution of Expected Inflation and Output Growth" *Journal of Economic Literature*, November 2002.

24 Source–*Fortune*. Accessed July 2, 2015, at http://fortune.com/2011/02/01/bernankes-biggest-blunders/

- On national television Jim Cramer advised investors: "I have thought about this all weekend…Whatever money you need for the next five years, please take it out of the stock market right now."[25] This was said October 8, 2008 on the Today Show. An investor who took his advice and sold that day would have missed out on 84 percent appreciation over the next five years.[26]

To be fair, stock market "experts" get it right sometimes. The problem is the correct predictions tend to be a prediction of the status quo, meaning there is no material benefit to their predictions. But when they get it wrong, it often has costly consequences. So following "expert" forecasts has very little upside and a lot of downside. That is not an attractive payoff.

It's not that these experts lack intelligence. It's just that their world is unpredictable. The unreliability of predictions is really important because forecasters are always making predictions. Those predictions tell our brain that the market is predictable, that future market and economic outcomes can be known.

"The question is not whether these people are well-trained. It is whether their world is predictable."[27]

—Daniel Kahneman

25 Inbar, Michael. "Jim Cramer: Time to get out of the stock market." Retrieved August 8, 2015, at http://www.today.com/id/27045699/ns/today-money/t/jim-cramer-time-get-out-stock-market/#.VcYyXGDtk2w

26 Returns are of the S&P 500 from October 7, 2008, through October 7, 2013. Dividends reinvested.

27 Kahneman, Daniel. *Thinking, Fast & Slow.* ©2011. Farrar, Straus and Giroux, New York. Page 221.

The hard truth is that the market and the economy are unpredictable. The evidence of that is that people can't accurately predict it. Sure, someone will get it right once in a while. But even a broken clock is correct twice per day. There is no consistency. It doesn't matter how many Ph.D.'s you have and how many years of experience, you can't project where the ball will stop on the roulette wheel. Your prediction is going to be as good as mine, because the nature of the game is random and unpredictable.

Finding A Better Forecast

How do we identify a better forecaster? Are some better than others?

Yes. According to Philip Tetlock, accurate forecasters tend to take ideas from other areas, so they have multiple disciplines built in. They also accept errors in their forecasts and recognize that they have made errors before. They recognize that the world is complex and uncertain, so their forecasts may include qualifying words, such as, "We think with such degree of uncertainty or probability." They base their forecasts more on observation than on theory.[28]

---

28 Silver, Nate. *The Signal and the Noise.* ©2012. Penguin Books. New York.

Less-accurate forecasts usually have a very concentrated focus without considering other disciplines or other fields of intelligence. They also tend to deflect blame and responsibility such as, "My forecast would have been right if investors acted rationally."

Poor forecasts tend to be very confident and precise: "This is what is going to happen, and this is why it is going to happen." They also tend to be ideological and theoretical: "Had these uncertain events not occurred, my prediction would have come to pass." The problem is that our future contains many uncertain events.

So is it wise to heed financial forecasts and use them to help us make better investment decisions? James Montier, a member of GMO's asset allocation team, opined: "It would be sheer madness to base an investment process around our seriously flawed ability to divine the future."[29]

The illusions of certainty are also fueled by inferences of causation—cause and effect. The brain loves cause and effect because it provides clarity and certainty. It tells us why something happened. We say to ourselves, A caused B. So in the future, when I see A, I know that B will occur. Many times, when two events are correlated or happen simultaneously, we incorrectly judge one as having caused another.

Every morning, a child in his bed on the farm hears the rooster crow. Shortly thereafter, the sun rises. The child thinks, therefore, the rooster causes the sun to rise.

His older sister, on the other hand, wise in the ways of the world, has more information and knows otherwise. As investors, oftentimes our perspective may be as limited as the young child's.

29 Montier, James. *The Little Book of Behavioral Investing.* ©2010. John Wiley & Sons, New Jersey. Page 60.

We have some information but do not see the big picture. What looks like cause and effect may in reality be two events that tend to occur about the same time with no *causal* connection. Superstition is a result of inferring a causal relationship where none exists.

A friend of mine is a die-hard Green Bay Packers fan. Sometimes he will choose not to watch their playoff games because when he has watched in the past, they have lost. His watching, of course, doesn't affect the performance of the Packers or their opponents. His faulty logic has evolved into superstition, which cheats my friend out of watching his favorite team at the most crucial part of the season.

Our desire to identify cause and effect leads us to believe the past was inevitable. This is further exacerbated by the fact that everything makes sense in hindsight. "Of course that happened. Now I see it." That thinking will lead us to believe the future is more predictable than it really is, further making us victim to the illusion of certainty.

The economy and market are so complex, with so many different inputs, we cannot be sure exactly what causes a certain outcome or maxim. We may have an intuition that seems right, but we really don't know. If we can recognize the difference between when one event causes another and when events are independent of each other, we may avoid a bad investment choice down the road.

The next time you are influenced to make investment decisions based on an individual's (or consensus) forecast, ask yourself what if the exact *opposite* happened. This is actually quite important because some of the most costly forecasting errors are because the opposite happened. For instance, in 2008, one Mad

Money viewer asked whether he should be concerned about Bear Stearns and sell.

Jim Cramer said, "No! No! No! Bear Stearns is fine. Do not take your money out. Bear Stearns is not in trouble. If anything, they're more likely to be taken over. Don't move your money from Bear. That's just being silly. Don't be silly."[30] One week later, Bear Stearns collapsed. A total loss. There are many other examples of "experts" getting their prediction dead wrong.

If you are expecting strong growth and position your portfolio accordingly, what would happen if there was a recession instead? What if you were expecting a recession and we had strong growth? If you were to follow the expert prediction and it was wrong, how much would your portfolio suffer? Let us remember that market experts tend to predict many more recessions that never occur, and don't seem to predict those crises that do occur.

---

30 Retrieved August 8, 2015, at http://www.moneybluebook.com/cnbcs-jim-cramer-advises-investors-bear-stearns-is-fine-dont-be-silly/

Key Takeaways

1. Our brain desires certainty and oftentimes can be fooled by the illusion of certainty provided in market and economic forecasts.

2. Experts have a poor track record of accurately predicting market and economic events because of the unpredictability of the market.

3. Our search for cause and effect exacerbates the illusion of certainty by tricking us into believing that the future is more predictable than it really is.

4. When considering a forecast, be sure to also consider the effect if the opposite occurred.

My Notes

Chapter Five

The Illusion of Control

Randomness is one of the great consistencies in life.

The inability of experts to consistently predict economic and market outcomes is evidence that the market is unpredictable. In other words, it is random, especially over the short term.

We don't know when the market is going to go up or when it is going to go down. We don't know by what magnitude it will move or for how long. Indeed, the outcome will be random for us. It will only be after the event that we may identify a cause and effect, but that doesn't do the investor any good.

We are uncomfortable with the word "random." If something is random, we cannot control the outcomes. And we want to *feel* in control.

We often detect patterns in random outcomes. While this is obvious when flipping a coin, it is not so when dealing with investments. We often attribute skill (or lack thereof) to random outcomes.

Let's take the example of a mutual fund that is performing better than its peers and the index it tracks. We may think:

"That's because the portfolio manager is so good. I'm going to buy some of that." But no mutual fund manager outperforms all of the time. The market is random, especially over the short term.

If the markets were not random, and our investment returns were totally dependent upon our skill, then why would a portfolio manager outperform for one period of time and underperform for another? Would he not choose to outperform all of the time?

When you flip a coin, which outcome is more likely?

HHTHT or HHHHH

Most people would choose the first example because our brain expects variation within random outcomes. The first example looks random. The second looks made up, or at least very rare. But each outcome has the same three percent probability.

We know that most casino games are dominated by random outcomes. Slot machines, roulette, and war require zero skill whatsoever. And yet people who play those games and are winning are said to be "hot." When a slot machine happens to be paying out frequently, it attracts attention because it is "hot." Someone winning a significant amount of hands in blackjack is "on a roll." Yet all these outcomes are normal because, in the short term, random outcomes can trend; they can appear non-random.

The same is said for investments and investment managers. Mutual fund managers who have good prior performance compared to the crowd attract significantly more money than their more "average" peers. Yet their outperformance likely has to do with luck … even if it is over a long period of time. If their outperformance were truly skillful, they would never underperform. Flip a coin 10 times in a row and record the outcome. Repeat the exercise numerous times. You are eventually going to get a series of 10 heads or 10 tails. While that outcome may be unlikely, if you do it long it enough it will occur. That is the nature of randomness.

Micromanaging Investments

Many investors micromanage their portfolio. They feel better if they're doing something because it makes them *feel* that they are in control. This is the illusion of control. An investor may think: "If I constantly monitor my investments, I can make adjustments that will help me achieve a greater return."

That may hold true for a few investors, but the great majority of investors are influenced to do the wrong thing at the wrong time. They have the best of intentions: protect on the downside and profit on the upside.

But because market movements are random in a short term, we don't know what to make of it. We don't know whether the next correction will be a great buying opportunity or the first step to much greater losses until well after the fact.

Review the following chart and consider why both stock and bond investors significantly underperformed their respective index in 2014.

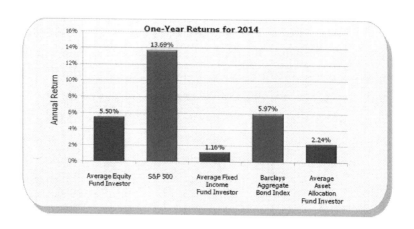

Why do you think the average stock investor underperformed the S&P 500 in 2014?

While we cannot know for sure, we can make an educated guess. Based on my experience in traveling the country and speaking with financial advisors and retail investors, I believe a contributing factor to the underperformance may have been the Ebola scare in the fall of 2014.

Ebola was all over the news for more than a week. The media showed images of people in full-body medical suits working with the victims. It was so significant that President Obama even named an "Ebola czar."

The media craze began in early October and was over as quickly as it started. The S&P 500 index dropped precipitously as the media coverage increased. Many investors, wanting to protect the downside, made some adjustments to their portfolio by selling stocks.

Within two weeks, the market had recovered all of its losses, leaving those who sold stocks to recognize their error and await a correction so they could get back in. Those investors left the realm of investing and are now in the business of market timing. Good intentions; bad results.

Perhaps they decided that they couldn't take another 2008/2009 and did what they thought was best. But it turned out to be costly. That is the problem with micromanaging investments and focusing on short-term news and outcomes.

The fear of Ebola may have caused the market to go down, but who would have guessed it would end as quickly as it began? I don't think the newly appointed Ebola czar even had a chance to move to Washington, D.C.

In this case, the event that may have influenced investors to sell was random; Ebola—or any health scare—is unrelated to the market.

Why do you think the average bond investor underperformed so significantly in 2014?

Just like with stocks, we cannot know for sure. But 2014 was fraught with interest rate predictions and speculation. "When will the Fed raise rates?" "What will happen to the value of long-term bonds?" The talk was all about bond yields increasing, which causes bond prices to fall. Some well-intentioned bond investors may have acted on the near certainty of rising interest rates. Except rates went down in 2014, which caused bond prices to increase.

It appears that faulty predictions and investors with good intentions (but no set strategy) may have been a contributing factor to the significant underperformance both stock and bond investors experienced in 2014. Micromanaging a portfolio may seem smart, but because of the random and unpredictable nature of the markets it may result in costly outcomes.

Skill vs. Luck

Randomness is systemic. The market as a system is random. Luck is individual. I was lucky to buy this security right before it went up.

When it comes to investing, we have a hard time determining what is skill and what is luck because of our innate desire to identify cause and effect. When we recognize our inability to consistently pinpoint causal relationships in investing, then we can get a better idea how much luck is involved in an investment scheme, which may help us make better decisions.

Skill ←————————————————————————————→ Luck

Market returns aren't entirely driven by luck. There certainly is some skill involved. On a continuum, with pure luck on one side and pure skill on the other, investing is somewhere in between. We can all pick the best stocks in the world, but if the market goes down, we will likely lose money, such as we lost in '08 and '09. On the flip side, if we buy some of the worst stocks and have a very favorable market, we will likely make money, such as in 1999. That is the element of luck.

Since we would like more control over our investment returns, what can we do to increase the role of skill when it comes to investing? Activities that involve a degree of luck or randomness, such as investing, require many outcomes to get to the average. Therefore, one of the elements of skill in investing is the ability to be patient. Flip the coin only five times, and you may get all heads. Flip a coin a thousand times, and you will have roughly half heads and half tails.

If the market goes up on average, then we need to give it enough time for the average to occur.

That can mean waiting longer than we would like. Because the market is random, what worked yesterday may not work tomorrow. Asset classes, sectors, and strategists go in and out of favor. Many investors chase what is hot today, whether it be a stock, fund, or exchange traded fund (ETF). I call this "strategy chasing." It is very difficult to own securities that are doing poorly, especially when other securities are doing so well. The temptation to abandon the current holdings is very strong. The fact that the media is talking about it *ad nauseam* and most everyone is doing it makes the urge to abandon our investment strategies very strong. System 1 is responding. We need to give time for System 2 to engage.

In addition to patience, another skill to investing is to be persistent with our strategy, despite the urges and feelings to act right away. This assumes, of course, that we have a strategy. When it comes to investing, the process we identify as best for ourselves is going to be what we should follow. If we don't have a defined process, there is nothing to refer to, and acting on impulse may be more likely.

Warren Buffett missed out on huge gains in 1999 because the opportunities didn't fit his investment strategy. Specifically, his strategy is that he must understand the company, and he said he didn't understand technology. For a period, many viewed him as out of touch. But he didn't deviate from his process, and it ended up being very profitable for him.

Create your investment plan, define your process, and stick to it. I define and discuss how to construct an investment plan in Chapter 11. My hope is by the time you get to that point, you will realize *why* you need one.

A process may take time to demonstrate that it is paying off. The right process can look awful in the short term because of bad luck. The wrong process can look great in the short term thanks to good luck. Don't let short-term outcomes define whether your process is successful. Sometimes great investments and strategies (such as Buffett's in 1999) can perform terribly over some periods of time. (See the graphs in Chapter Three.)

Key Takeaways

1. The random nature of the markets, and our innate desire to control outcomes, leads to the illusion of control that influences investment decisions.

2. Micromanaging our investments and making decisions based on short-term outcomes often results in costly outcomes.

3. True investment skill is not in selecting a specific security or getting in at the right time. Real skill is to (i) define your investment strategy, (ii) be patient with the strategy, and (iii) stick with the strategy through thick and thin.

My Notes

Chapter Six

News and Noise

"Anyone who listens to news (except when very, very significant events take place) is one step below a sucker."[31]

—Nassim Taleb

Most investors want to be informed about market and economic events, whether it is for their own investment decisions or so they can answer a question knowledgeably and be in the know. We have lots of sources to which we can turn for information, and news organizations compete for our attention. Reporters and analysts for financial news organizations spew out breaking news, headlines, and data as if every word out of their mouth were crucial to our existence.

One thing we need to be aware of is the difference between news and noise. News contains the limited information that is actually material to our decision-making process. Noise is everything else they report. Of course, the more we listen to the news, the more noise fills our minds. It's a numbers game.

---

31 Taleb, Nassim Nicholas. *Antifragile: Things That Gain From Disorder.* ©2012. Random House. New York. Kindle Location 2399.

News organizations must fill their allotted time and space, whether it's TV or radio or printed pages or web pages, regardless of the amount of actual news that is happening at any given time.

Nassim Taleb, a scholar and bestselling author whose work has focused on probability and randomness, has said that a newspaper "should be of two-line length on some days, 200 pages on others,"[32] based upon the amount of actual news that's occurring that day.

That would benefit the reader, but not the media organization. The media, like every other for-profit entity, is in business to make money. They make money primarily from selling advertising. Since they cannot have a 30-minute program with nothing but commercials, or a newspaper with nothing but ads, they must fill airtime and pages with news. Some days there is plenty of news; other days news is scarce, and editors are forced to broadcast stories that aren't really news … just noise. But since viewers and readers aren't aware the editors are only filling time and space, they think the noise is important.

If no one tunes in or buys a newspaper, the news organizations won't survive. There's an incredible amount of effort and thought put into making sure you not only tune into the news, but that you tune into that particular news program. This is because they compete with each other. For every minute of valuable information, such as an interview with a CEO of a company, there are several minutes of noise.

In 2015, Brian Williams was suspended for six months and ultimately lost his job as trusted anchor for NBC News because he had embellished his role in some stories. Sensationalism is a major part of the news today, especially among the financial me-

---

32   Ibid. Kindle Location 2410.

dia. Most news is boring. Who would tune into something boring? It must be made exciting. It needs to be more interesting than other media outlets or the viewer will change the channel.

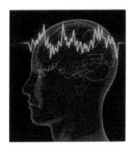

Mind Games: Tricks our Mind Plays with Respect to Money, and How to Win With the Proper Perspective

Thanks to a nationwide speaking contract, I spent a good portion of 2015 traveling coast to coast, speaking to groups of retail investors just like you and me. I presented "Mind Games" more than 200 times in a span of nine months to thousands of investors. The presentation discusses how to gain a better perspective by understanding several ways our brain tricks us. These mental shortcuts and our emotions influence many of our investment decisions.

My favorite part of the presentation is when we discuss the media, its primary role and how it subconsciously influences our decisions. While we may consciously tune in to be informed, there are many subconscious factors that influence us to make poor investment decisions. I always ask the crowd to provide tactics they have seen the television medium employ to get people to tune in. Here are some of the most common responses:

Sensationalism. Making a story grander than it really is. Without this, most news is boring and not material. Without sensationalism, we may become disinterested and tune out (which is exactly what we should do).

Emotion. Constant countdowns to some arbitrary and short-term data such as an index hitting a new high, stocks hitting new lows, or dissecting a quote from Janet Yellen.

Volume. Reporters like to shout when markets are volatile. Since volatility is an inherent nature of financial markets, why do they need to shout? They are masters of getting our attention.

Urgency. The constant movement on the screen, even something as simple as running ticker tape at the bottom. The constant updates on markets create an illusion of anticipation and action. It gives us the sense that we need to do something, or we will miss out.

Certainty. They interview experts who will tell us which way the market is heading, usually with a focus on short-term outcomes. For example, I recently saw a panel of experts discussing: "What will move the markets next week?" The fact is, they don't know. The market is unpredictable in the short-term, and experts are wrong more often than right. So they present a damaging illusion of certainty.

Short-termism. All of these tactics and others influence us to pay attention to short-term outcomes. This makes sense. If you are really a long-term investor, you do not care about the market today or tomorrow—there is no need for you to tune in. So they must get you thinking short term so you will tune in today, tomorrow, and beyond. But the shorter term we think, the worse we do as investors.

We are Hardwired to Believe

One of the great "games" of the mind is that the more we hear of something, the more we believe it is true or likely to happen. In other words, whatever we are listening to can change our opinion and therefore our decision/behavior. And the more we hear it, the more we can be influenced.

We also can be influenced based on how easy (or difficult) something is to imagine. One of the greatest challenges about predicting "black swans" is that it is near impossible to predict something we have never experienced before. Creating scenarios that have never happened before are usually deemed "impossible". Even if such a prediction were made, most people would discount the prediction because what we haven't experienced before seems unlikely to happen.

Everything that has ever happened, at one point had never happened.

Things that are familiar or on the top of our mind may seem very likely to happen. Think about the financial crisis of 2008/2009. After such a significant crisis, there are many people just waiting for the next one. It's not a question of whether there will be another financial collapse, the question is when it will occur. This is the same for whatever story the media is focusing on that day, whether it be Ebola, interest rates, Greece, China or yesterday's stock market move.

Whatever the media is talking about today may influence our future investment decisions. And the more they talk about it, the more it can influence us–if we pay attention. But we need to remember the media exists for ratings, not to help us reach our financial goals. If you feel influenced to make an investment decision based on the news story of the day, it may be best to delay your decision, find out how such a decision affects your investment plan and perhaps speak with a trusted individual to ensure that your decisions are based on thoughtful analysis, and not a short-term, emotional response to the "noise" of the day.

Key Takeaways

1. Recognize the media uses tactics to get you to tune in, and those tactics may influence you to think and act based on short-term outcomes.

2. Additional information (such as today's news and stock quotation) is not always of value and may be detrimental to your portfolio.

3. If you are influenced to make a change, ask yourself, "Where did this idea originate?" If it originated from the financial media, viewer beware.

4. Discussing your decisions with a trusted third party (such as a financial advisor) *before* acting on them may help improve your decision-making process.

My Notes

Chapter Seven

A Pat on the Back

"The road to investing hell is paved with overconfidence."[33]

—Jason Zweig

Confidence is essential to success. Even overconfidence sometimes will work in our favor: it can give us the courage to ask for that raise, quit our job for another, or start a family. It helps us progress in life. But when it comes to investing, overconfidence can lead to costly mistakes. The propensity is to take ownership of the good things that happen and to deflect blame when bad things happen. Over time, we tell ourselves how good we are without balancing it out with all the errors and bad decisions we have made. This causes us to become more confident in our abilities than we really should be.

Let's say you purchased a security. Six months later, it goes up 70 percent. What are you telling yourself? "I am a great investor." "I did the research and knew this was going up." "My instincts don't lie."

---

33 Zweig, Jason. *Your Money & Your Brain.* ©2007. Simon & Schuster. New York. Page 118.

On the other hand, let's say you purchased a security, and it goes down 70 percent over the next six months. Whose fault is that? You may say it's the company's fault, it's the market's fault, it's somebody's fault, but it certainly isn't your fault.

In my presentations, I often ask who in the room is a better-than-average driver. The majority of the hands go up … at least three-fourths of the room. When I ask who is worse than average, only a few hands go up. Sometimes it's as few as two or three in the crowd of 100. This is a popular psychological question, and the results demonstrate that we believe we are better drivers than is statistically possible. We are overconfident in our driving abilities. Having said that, I still think I am a better than average driver … and you probably think that as well.

> The one thing that unites all human beings, regardless of age, gender, religion, economic status or ethnic background, is that, deep down inside, we ALL believe that we are above average drivers.
>
> - Dave Barry

Overconfidence, Nassim Taleb says, is when "people overvalue their knowledge and underestimate the probability of their being wrong."[34]

Overconfidence is fueled by optimism. It's fueled by unrealistic optimism. Meir Statman, a professor of finance at Santa Clara University, found that unrealistic optimism leads investors to believe they are better than others when they, in fact, are not. Those investors tend to favor concentrated positions rather than a diversified portfolio.[35] They become so confident and optimistic about the future, they don't see how they can be wrong. They may purchase securities that increase the actual risk of the portfolio, but they don't recognize it.

It's not just investors who tend to be overconfident; it's also the experts. What's interesting is that we actually prefer people who are confident to people who are accurate. Psychologists have found that not only do people prefer those who sound confident, but also people are willing to pay more for confident-but-inaccurate advisers.[36] Perhaps this is because confident individuals provide the illusion of certainty that we so much desire.

One study in which professionals were 100 percent confident in their stock picks found that they were right less than 12 per-

34   Taleb, Nassim Nicholas. *Fooled by Randomness.* ©2004. Random House, New York. Page 210.

35   Statman, Meir. *What Investors Really Want.* ©2011. McGraw-Hill. New York.

36   Price, PC & Stone, ER. 2004. "Intuitive Evaluation of Likelihood Judgment Producers: Evidence for a Confidence Heuristic," *Journal of Behavioral Decision Making*, 17, Pages 39—57.

cent of the time. The biggest factor that led to such surety was "other knowledge that they had."[37]

Another study found that information increases confidence, but not necessarily accuracy.[38] There is a lot of information that helps us *feel* confident about our choices, but we need to recognize that an abundance of information is not necessarily making us more accurate, just more confident in our choices.

"True wisdom and judgment come from understanding our limitations when it comes to thinking about the future."[39]

—Frank Partnoy.

Given our propensity to believe we are better investors than we really are, it is important to recognize our limitations. This is not just about investors, but the same limitations hold true for the experts. We can make better decisions by recognizing investor skill is not about predicting the future, rather it's about ignoring the noise, taking advantage of the volatility and sticking to our strategy.

---

37   Torngren G & Montgomery H. 2004. "Worse Than Chance? Performance and Confidence among Professionals and Laypeople in the Stock Market," *Journal of Behavioral Finance*, 5.

38   Montier, James. *Little Book of Behavioral Investing*. ©2010 John Wiley & Sons. New Jersey. Page 76. as cited in Tsai, C, Klayman, J & Hastie, R. 2007. "Effects of Amount of Information on Judgment Accuracy and Confidence." Working Paper.

39   Partnoy, Frank. *Wait: The Art and Science of Delay.* ©2012. PublicAffairs, New York. Page 244.

As we learned in Chapter 1, we are influenced to be unrealistically optimistic and overconfident thanks to the influence of dopamine. A profitable trade can trigger a release of dopamine, which gives us feelings of confidence, optimism, and even invincibility. This could ultimately lead us to take on more risks than we can handle because we don't see the downside. We *feel* things will go our way; there is no way we can be wrong. But in an uncertain scheme such as investing, we should never be too sure of anything.

That is why it is imperative that we recognize the limits of what we know and can predict. When you are evaluating a forecast, it may be helpful to consider a greater range of potential outcomes—including outcomes that are undesirable (such as negative performance).

"What counts for most people in investing is not how much they know but rather how realistically they define what they don't know."[40]

—Warren Buffett.

Recognizing the Error

It is also important that we learn from our investment mistakes. If we don't accept and learn from our mistakes, we're bound to

---

40 "Chairman's Letter," 1992 Berkshire Hathaway Inc. annual report located at www.berkshirehathaway.com/letters/1992.html

repeat them. Some questions we should ask as we reflect on our mistakes include:

- What was the trigger that led me to make the mistake?
- Was I influenced by the media?
- Did I follow a forecast from an expert that was wrong?
- Was it a tip from a friend?
- Was I influenced by short-term performance?
- Did market volatility influence my action?

It is crucial to discover exactly what the trigger was that led you to make a bad investment decision. Once you've identified that, the next step is to identify a better outcome. Given the trigger in the situation, what would have been a more desirable outcome for you? This is straightforward, because when it comes to investing, the outcome is usually either greater return or less risk. Identify your primary desire and make a plan to *behave* better next time.

What will you do the next time you feel that same impulse, the next time you get an idea to act right away? Physiologically, you will want to do something. In this case, we want to replace a hasty decision with something more productive. Let's illustrate with a story.

David heard negative reports on a stock and noticed his investment was losing money. So he sold the stock, which he had purchased just one month ago. He later realized the loss was temporary, and the stock had increased to a much higher price than the price at which he had sold it. David made an investment mistake. We all have. Now he needs to learn from it.

David needs to realize why he purchased the stock in the first place. He had been hearing about the stock for some time and thought it would make a lot of money. He didn't put much thought into what to expect from the stock except that it would make him money. When it started losing money, and the media reported negative things about it, he panicked and sold the stock.

The media was the trigger to buy and sell the stock. A better outcome for David would have been to avoid the impulsive investment decision and to ignore the chatter of the media.

To correct this going forward, David may want to create a plan for investing in which he defines specific parameters for stocks to buy and sell. The parameters provide the "why" for buying or selling a security, rather than "just to make money." He may also benefit from engaging a financial professional to help him avoid impulsive decisions, ignore the noise, and provide discipline to his plan.

The tragedy isn't the mistake. The tragedy is failing to learn from the mistake.

How Could I Be Wrong?

Whenever we are evaluating a security to purchase or sell, it is important we consider how we could be wrong *before* we take action. Evaluating ways in which a security may lose money is not a desirable task, but it is a necessary part of a thoughtful investment plan. This is especially true for securities that have very high-growth potential and high valuations.

No investor is correct 100 percent of the time, therefore it is important to understand how you could be wrong, and what it may cost you. For every security transaction, there is a buyer and a seller. As you are confident in the future gains of a given security, another investor is not, and chooses to sell it to you. One of you is going to be wrong.

A pro/con list may be helpful when evaluating securities. The pros are the ways in which the company is going to do great, and the cons are ways in which the company may not do as well as expected. And be realistic with your analysis. There are always reasons a company may not do as well as expected, such as new competition, a change in tax laws or government regulation, an economic downturn, etc. Remember that a great company does not always translate into a great stock and vice versa.

Key Takeaways

① Investor optimism and overconfidence cause us to underestimate investment risk and take more risk than we are comfortable with.

② Increased information breeds excessive confidence, but doesn't necessarily result in better decisions.

③ Investors need to recognize the limits of their ability (and that of experts)—including the ability to accurately predict future security prices.

④ Identifying and remembering past mistakes can help us improve our decision-making skills in the future.

⑤ Create a pro/con list when evaluating securities and consider the cost of being wrong.

My Notes

Chapter Eight

Reference Points to the Rescue

"Starting points have a profound impact on ending points."[41]

—Daniel Gilbert

Watching my then-8-year-old son play soccer was a frustrating activity. Here are a bunch of boys congregated around this ball, all 10 of them, as if the ball were the nucleus and they were protons and electrons circling it. Parents were told by the soccer league not to yell instructions from the sidelines; just let the boys play. I couldn't help myself. I would yell for my son to move away 10 to 15 feet and wait for a pass, or at least for the ball to come loose. He would do it for about 10 seconds and then go right back to the ball as if gravity sucked him in.

During halftime, I would remind him to spread out. But it is almost instinctive of us to go to where things are happening, or just happened, rather than anticipate where things will happen. I wanted my son to learn some Wayne Gretzky wisdom: don't go to where the puck (ball) is; rather, go to where the puck (ball) will

---

41 Gilbert, Daniel. *Stumbling on Happiness.* ©2006. Vintage Books. New York. Page 149.

be. Mission not accomplished. The instinct is to go where things are now. "The now" is one type of reference point. And reference points influence us, consciously or subconsciously.

The Influence of Reference Points

Did you know that Germany won the World Cup in 2014? Germany has always had a good soccer team. The German team has dominated the U.S. soccer team for years, even though the U.S. has a much larger pool of potential soccer players to choose from. The United States has a population of 320 million; Germany's population is only 82 million.

Humor me by providing your best, educated guess to this question.

What is the temperature of the sun at its core in Fahrenheit?

A. 27 million

B. 54 million

C. 71 million

D. 88 million

Do you have your answer? Great! I love asking this question. What is so interesting is that when I ask the question when I am making a presentation, the majority of the audience answers either 71 million or 88 million. When I say the majority, I mean at least 70 percent of the attendees.

On the contrary, less than 10 percent guess 27 million. Why such a wide gap on a question that most people don't know? You would expect the answers to be more evenly dispersed based on random guessing. The reason is that responses are not random; they are influenced by a reference point.

If you answered 71 or 88, I ask, "What does the temperature of the sun have to do with the population of Germany?"

Of course, it has nothing to do with it, but in this case, the populations of Germany and the U.S. subconsciously influence people to guess high numbers. The correct answer to the question is 27 million degrees Fahrenheit. How do I know that is the correct temperature? No, I have not yet visited the core of the sun. I simply searched it on Google.

Here is another example of the power of reference points, this time from a study done by behavioral economics pioneers Daniel Kahneman and Amos Tversky.[42]

There's a wheel of fortune with numbers from 0 to 100. Participants were asked to spin the wheel and write the number it landed on. What the participants didn't know was that the wheel was rigged to stop at either 10 or 65. Those would be the only two possible numbers they could write. (Those are the reference points.)

Then they were asked this question: "What is your best guess of the percentage of African nations in the UN?" Those who spun a "10" had an average guess of 25 percent. Those who spun a "65" had an average guess of 45 percent. Clearly they were influenced by a wheel of fortune that had nothing to do with the question at hand.

It's amazing how this works. When we're asked a question to which we do not know the answer, the brain will seek a reference point or starting point from which to formulate a response. This occurs not only when we are asked to provide a response to a

---

42   Kahneman, Daniel. *Thinking, Fast & Slow*. ©2011. Farrar, Straus and Giroux, New York. Page 119.

question to which we don't know the answer, but also when we are asked to make inferences about the future. If we don't know what the future will hold, we are often influenced by the recent past. The recent past becomes the reference point for our estimate of future outcomes.

Economic and market predictions of the future look eerily similar to what recently just happened. Forecasts tend to mirror the past. One study by GMO found that "analysts are exceptionally good at one thing, and possibly one thing alone—telling you what has just happened."[43]

In a different study, researchers examined 2,000 past economic predictions and found that economists didn't predict anything. Their prediction was just an extrapolation of prior data.[44]

This is not too surprising because neuroscientists have found that remembering and imagining the future occur at the same place in the brain. Through functional MRI (fMRI), researchers have seen that the same neural networks light up when we remember the past and imagine the future.[45]

Reference Points and Feelings

Reference points work not only for data but also for our feelings. We use our present feelings as a starting point for how we are likely to feel in the future.

43 Montier, James. *The Little Book of Behavioral Investing.* ©2010. John Wiley & Sons, New Jersey. Page 108.

44 Bouchaud, J.P., & Potters, M. 2003. "Theory of financial risks and derivatives pricing: from statistical physics to risk management." 2nd ed. Cambridge, MA. Cambridge University Press.

45 Kellogg, Ronald T. *Making of the Mind.* ©2013. Prometheus Books. New York. Kindle Location 2193.

If we shop for groceries after a heavy meal, we're likely to buy less than if we shop when we are hungry. Similarly with the market, if we're bullish and optimistic today, those feelings may cause us to believe the future will be very good. This explains why we like to buy securities after prices have gone up. Upon experiencing gains, the dopamine is released, which increases our optimism and confidence.

We project our current mood into the future. We don't see how things can deteriorate, so we buy high with the expectation that things are going much higher. On the flip side, we may project negative feelings well into the future, leading us to sell assets at low prices today. When we experience losses, we often experience anxiety and fear, and the amygdala may be activated. The future will not appear promising.

We may ask: What will the market do this year? What will the value of my portfolio be next year? Will I be able to retire and maintain my lifestyle for the rest of my life? These are all questions that we do not have an answer for. Because we don't know the answer to these future outcomes, our minds may be susceptible to subconsciously seeking out reference points. There are many types of reference points, but perhaps the most common reference point is past performance.

Reference Points and Performance

We love purchasing securities based upon past performance because the brain has detected a pattern of performance and projects that performance into the future. It tells us subconsciously that the past performance is a predictor of future performance.

Companies that sell mutual funds know this. When you see an advertisement for a mutual fund, what is it advertising? The manager's philosophy or their buy-and-sell discipline? No. The fund is touting past performance, how they compare to other funds (Lipper), or their Morningstar Rating (all of which are based on past performance).

When was the last time you saw a 1-star or 2-star rated mutual fund being advertised? I don't think I've ever seen that. (The Morningstar Rating is a scale of 1-5, so one or two stars is not good.) Empirical evidence shows that a good Morningstar rating attracts money … a lot of money. And a bad rating results in negative fund flows. A study by Financial Research Corporation found that in 1999, firms with 4 or 5 stars increased their assets by $233 billion while lower-rated funds had investors withdraw $132 billion.[46]

While everyone else is running toward the soccer ball—in other words, buying whatever security is "hot" today—it is important for investors to take a step back and assess the situation with a greater perspective. System 1 is about acting on instinct; this is about overriding System 1 and acting on thoughtful consideration of possible future outcomes.

Reference Points and Risk

We (individually) have no power over the performance of the stock market. When we purchase a security, we are hoping it will perform well, but we are subject to what all other investors, speculators and high-frequency traders do. Let's face it: we have no control over the return, but we do have control over the risk of the portfolio. Many risky assets have done very well over the past several years, yet they did horribly in 2008-2009.

---

46 Reichenstein, William. "Morningstar's New Star-Rating System: Advances and Innovations." *Journal of Financial Planning*. March 2004.

The constant is risk and volatility—securities (and the market as a whole) go up and down quite a bit. The unknown is when the risk will work in our favor (positive returns) and when it will work against us (negative returns). It is important that we calculate both the upside and downside potential of securities.

A recent *Wall Street Journal* article, "The New Era of Low Stock Returns," analyzed expected payoffs in the stock market based upon certain metrics.[47] Economist Robert Shiller, using his P/E (Price to Earnings) valuation method and comparing it to historical performance of similar valuations levels, believes annual stock returns may average 2.5 percent over the next ten years. Another method estimates stock returns at 3.5 percent per year.

Will these estimates be accurate? I have no clue and neither do you. While the past does not guarantee what the future will be, sometimes it can act as a guide. So while you are chasing risk assets, you may want to ask yourself whether the payoff is worth it in the first place.

47   Zweig, Jason. "The Era of Low Stock Returns." Retrieved August 6, 2015, at http://blogs.wsj.com/moneybeat/2015/03/27/the-new-era-of-low-stock-returns/

Reference Points and Expectations

Let's say you have a financial plan done. The plan identifies your current situation, desired goals and provides required returns to achieve your goals over a given time period. Assume that the required rate of return is 7 percent, and the plan suggests a portfolio of securities that is expected to earn 7 percent or more over time. We assume that 7 percent long-term return is both reasonable and realistic.

The 7 percent now becomes the reference point. That isn't bad, but it isn't good either. If you are expecting 7 percent per year, on average, what does that really mean? It means you are expecting 7 percent each year (or better). What happens if the market is down 20 percent? You are shocked. While you know markets go up and down, you didn't even consider this. After all, why would a portfolio that is expected to earn 7 percent lose 20 percent in a year? This is the crux of the problem.

Reference points based on past returns or future expected returns, even if they are realistic, mask the inherent volatility of the markets. The brain will automatically and subconsciously use past or expected performance as a reference point. But we need to consciously provide additional reference points to consider such as, "What is the likely *range* of returns this portfolio will experience over the next few years?" Even if we obtain the 7 percent average return over the long term, it won't go straight up – there will be periods of losses along the way. So what *could* those losses be? If we aren't prepared to experience temporary losses, we may not be able to hang in there long enough to achieve our goals. We can tell the brain, upfront, what some potential outcomes are. If we provide a realistic range of returns we may experience during good and bad markets, we will be less likely to be shocked and jump ship when the unexpected occurs.

Key Takeaways

1. Next time you're searching for an expert to tell you when the market will turn, don't hold your breath. They're most likely going to "predict" what recently happened.

2. Feelings act as reference points when we imagine the future. It is wise not to make any investment changes during periods of heightened emotions such as excessive optimism or pessimism. We need a large dose of realism.

3. Your instinct is to repeat what just did well. Investment instincts are often wrong. Buy low and sell high often requires you to do the opposite of your instincts.

4. While we are instinctively influenced by past results, we should consciously engage System 2 to quantify how much risk is in the portfolio.

5. Be sure to consider the range of returns your portfolio is likely to experience over the course of a market cycle.

My Notes

Chapter Nine

The Pain of Loss

Most people feel the pain of loss more intensely then the joy from gain.

This year for Spring Break my family vacationed in Orlando, Florida. We were there for five days, and as part of the vacation, we had purchased a three-day pass to Disney World. We stayed at a resort that had several nice pools as well as activities for adults and kids. Our plan was to spend three days at Disney parks and the other two days at the hotel enjoying the pools, the sun, and the activities. As with most plans, sometimes changes need to be made on the fly to optimize the experience and outcome.

After spending two days at Disney parks and two days enjoying the resort pools, we discussed which Disney park we would visit on our last day, since we had purchased the three-day pass. It was then that we realized that none of us wanted to go to a Disney park again. We had a good time while we were at the parks, but the fantasy and expectation of going to Disney were more enjoyable than the actual experience.

The long lines, sea of people, and our kids' complaining about the lines and people made it difficult to have a "magical" day. After our Fastpasses had been used on the good rides, the only options were to wait 30 minutes for mediocre rides, watch the afternoon parade, and go to the Hall of Presidents. We did go to the Hall of Presidents, where I slept for about 20 minutes of the 22-minute presentation. I highly recommend it!

Normally this decision would be a no-brainer: obviously, if no one wants to go to Disney, we won't go. But we had already pre-purchased the third day. It was "free" to go to a Disney park. And not to go would mean that we just wasted $390 by purchasing a pass we didn't use. I do not like wasting money. This was the dilemma.

The moment we purchased the three-day Disney pass, it became a sunk cost. It was not refundable and could not be recovered in any way. It was clear what we wanted to do … stay at the resort. Yet, the potential of "throwing away money" made us think about whether we should do something we didn't want to do just so we didn't waste the money we had already spent.

We tend to feel the pain of loss more intensely than the joy of gaining something else. This is called loss aversion (a strong dislike of losing something). In this case, the loss was paying for a day at Disney, but not going. My aversion to paying for something I didn't use was causing us to irrationally consider doing something we didn't want to do (go to the park), rather than doing what we really wanted.

Ultimately, we decided to forgo Disney (and the ticket) for another day at the resort. But it wasn't an easy decision. No one likes to lose money or feel like they didn't get their money's worth. I believe the reason we were ultimately able to make the right decision in spite of the "lost money" was because we had aversions that were stronger than the pain and regret from losing money on the tickets. I had an aversion to the lines. I had an aversion to the sea of people. I had a strong aversion to hearing my kids complain. And I remembered from prior days' experience that, at least for us, the fantasy was better than the reality.

Now that we are several months past this experience, I can assure you we did the right thing. In fact, from this experience, I may be more likely to "throw money down the drain" in the future in order to have a better experience.

Loss Aversion in Investing

Loss aversion also influences investors. Loss aversion is driven by contempt for loss. It is fueled by the feelings of pride and regret. Loss aversion influences investors to sell their "winners" quickly while holding on to the "losers." Investors who seek the quick gain and allow the fear of loss to dominate their investment decisions earn substantially less than other investors. One study that analyzed thousands of past trades found that loss aversion had a "cost" of roughly 3.4 percent per year.[48]

However costly this strategy is, it is quite common among investors.

Loss aversion is more common when investing in individual securities compared to a basket of securities (i.e. market index, mutual fund). This may be because of the emotional attachment we may have to an individual security as well as the greater volatility in an individual security compared to a basket or fund consisting of many securities.

---

48 Odean, Terrance. "Are Investors Reluctant to Realize Their Losses?" *Journal of Finance*, Vol 53, No. 5, October 1998. Pages 1775-1997.

While we want to buy low and sell high, loss averse investors tend to sell quickly at a small gain (not very high) and tend to ride their losers until the loss is so great, the amygdala kicks in and they ultimately sell because they need to "get to safety." It is a financially costly, but emotionally appealing strategy.

Selling a winning investment is a psychological reward. It says you're a good investor, increases your confidence, and may even result in a shot of dopamine. Selling a losing investment is a double whammy. You're not just locking in your loss, but you also are taking this psychological hit from admitting you made a mistake. No one wants to lose money or admit a mistake. Instead, we tend to hold losing positions.

Many people hold losing investments just for the chance of one day breaking even. Decisions about buying and selling securities should be made based upon the future outlook of the security, not whether it is currently a gain or loss in your portfolio. If you had new cash to invest today, would you buy that same security (assuming you didn't own it)? If not, then why would you choose to hold it?

Are you loss averse?

A basic function of humans is to not want to lose, whether we are talking about money or a game. Losing something is accompanied by negative feelings, and we seek to avoid or at least minimize the loss. It would not be unrealistic to say all humans are averse to losing something.

Imagine you are faced with the following set of decisions. What would you choose for each one?

Decision 1. Choose Between: A) Sure gain of $240 B) 25 percent chance to gain $1,000 and 75 percent chance to gain nothing

Decision 2. Choose Between: C) Sure loss of $750 D) 75 percent chance to lose $1,000 and 25 percent chance to lose nothing

Responses A and D indicate loss aversion. In the original experiment authored by Kahneman and Tversky, which was of 150 participants, 73 percent of the participants chose A and D (loss aversion), and only 3 percent chose the statistically optimal combination of B and C.[49]

This same example can be updated with different dollar amounts to reflect today's conditions or the wealth of an individual, so long as the ratios remain the same.

Here is another example. John flips a coin. If it's heads, you owe John $1,000. If it's tails, John will pay you $ _____. What is the *least* amount of money John would have to pay you to play this game? (fill in the blank)

Any response at or above $2,000 indicates loss aversion, because you're requiring a payout of twice the potential loss. The larger the number, the greater the degree of loss aversion.

We are all averse to losses. The question is whether that aversion causes us to make poor decisions. When it comes to investing, there are a few things that investors who are significantly loss averse can do to help them stay the course.

49 Kahneman, Daniel. *Thinking, Fast & Slow.* ©2011. Farrar, Straus and Giroux, New York. Page 334.

Dealing with Loss Aversion

The following suggestions may be helpful in reducing the influence that loss aversion has on your investment decisions:

1) Construct a portfolio that includes assets other than stocks and bonds. Securities that move independently of the stock market are expected to moderate returns in good and bad markets, thus reducing the volatility of the portfolio. Lower volatility in portfolio returns may translate into less emotional volatility, thus less chance for loss aversion and the amygdala to kick in.

2) Another potential solution is to pay a premium in order to transfer some of the risk to another party. Some examples of this include the purchase of put options to temporarily protect the downside, or transferring your risk to an insurance company through the use of certain investment vehicles.

3) Another way to deal with loss aversion, which I had not thought about prior to my Disney experience, is to override loss aversion by identifying undesirable consequences that will result from the loss-averse action. If the undesirable consequences are strong enough (i.e. the stress of having to time the market to get back in), an aversion to those outcomes may be stronger than the aversion to temporary loss—allowing us to make a better decision.

So the question we should ask ourselves is: "What are some unintended and undesirable consequences of allowing loss aversion to influence my decisions?"

List a few undesirable consequences that will result directly from loss-averse behavior. For investors, undesirable outcomes may include lower returns, reduced quality of life in retirement, additional years to reach retirement, and/or additional stress from trading and timing the market.

If the aversion to undesirable outcomes is greater than the loss aversion, we may be able to make the less emotional and more thoughtful choice.

Key Takeaways

① Most investors have some degree of loss aversion. Find yours.

② Loss-averse behavior is a drag on portfolio performance.

③ Certain investment strategies may help reduce the negative consequences of loss aversion.

My Notes

_____

_____

_____

_____

_____

_____

Section 3

What You Can Do Now

Chapter Ten

What You See Is All There Is

"Perception is the basis of wisdom."[50]
— Edward de Bono

Perception is a point of view. It is our point of view, our reality. And perception drives our decisions. We form our perceptions through experience and current beliefs. If you want to understand why somebody behaves a certain way, you must understand his perception.

---

50 de Bono, Edward. *I Am Right - You Are Wrong.* ©1991. Penguin Books. New York. Page 27.

Perception can be wrong. If we are misremembering our experiences, or our current beliefs are misinformed, our perceptions and subsequent choices may not be in our best interest. If we make a lot of emotional and impulsive decisions that are detrimental to our well-being, we may want to back up and inspect our perceptions.

There are two primary reasons our perception could be wrong:

1) **Our current beliefs are wrong.** That could include incorrect stereotypes about investments, such as the idea that bonds are safe and stocks are risky. That is a common but incorrect stereotype.

   We may also have faulty logic such as: "My financial advisor should know what sector will outperform in the next year." Expecting a financial professional to know what's going to happen in the market is unrealistic.

   Or perhaps we attribute market movements to news or events, rather to just random occurrences. Take the market crash of 1987, known as Black Monday. Surely some negative news or event caused the market to lose more than 20 percent of its value in one day. You would think so, but that is not what happened. On Black Monday, there was no news, and there was no news prior to Black Monday either. The news that Monday was the fact that the market was crashing. That was the big news of the day.

2) **We tend to misremember the past.** This happens because our brain is not a hard drive. It does not save every single point and moment in life. Instead, it saves the gist of the event. When recalling an experience, the brain retrieves the "gist" and then has to fill in blanks. That "filling in" can be recent news, stereotypes, or other information floating around in

our head. We aren't remembering the exact event. We remember our memory of the event. Sometimes our memory of the event is incorrect.

It is not uncommon for an eyewitness to a crime to misidentify someone in a police lineup. Even though the witness is certain, he is remembering the memory of the event, not the event itself.

Perception of Performance

Many investors are tempted to abandon their investment strategy upon reviewing performance. Why? Because their perception of what is important to them has momentarily changed. They are no longer focusing on their personal goals; they are only interested in how they did relative to something else, such as a stock market index.

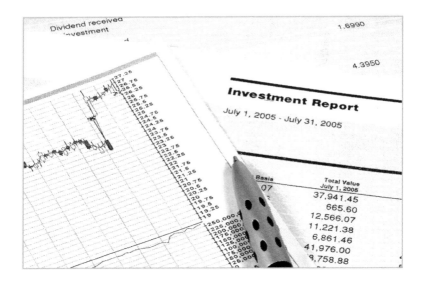

Let's say you are reviewing a statement of your investments. You notice your portfolio was up 7 percent for the year. Are you happy?

What if the market was up 21 percent during that period? Are you still happy? How did your neighbor do? What if your neighbor was up 33 percent during the same period? You probably wouldn't be too happy, and may very well reconsider your current strategy.

What if your neighbor took significantly more risk than you? Would you even think about risk, such as the fact that the market or your neighbor may be able to tolerate more risk than you? Or would you be too focused on how much money you *could* have had?

Most investors are working toward a long-term goal such as college funding, retirement, or building a legacy. But when we earn less than someone or something else, our perception may change. Our focus may switch from our retirement in 20 years to increasing our returns next month. We might say, "Sure. I was up 7 percent, and that is greater than I need to reach my personal goal, but I left a lot on the table. Should I not go more aggressive? That will enable me to reach my goals sooner."

The investor preference review on the following page may help you maintain the correct perception when you evaluate investment performance and remain focused on your long-term goals.

Investor Preference Review

It should be expected that we will be tempted to abandon our long-term goals. We are influenced by emotions and many illusions that cause us to act on short-term urges. Reflective questions, such as these, serve as a reminder of what our ultimate goals are.

❶ How important are peace of mind and security for your investment assets? (circle one)

1   2   3   4   5   6   7   8   9   10

Not important   Very important

❷ Which of the following is a more important goal for your investment portfolio?

☐ Manage Risk and Return   ☐ Maximize Return at Any Cost

❸ My primary objectives for investing are (select up to three):

☐ Beat the S&P 500 Index   ☐ Do Better than Others
☐ Financial Independence   ☐ College/Education Funding
☐ Comfortable Retirement   ☐ Build a Legacy
☐ Get Rich Quickly

❹ Which of the following does a stock index (i.e. S&P 500, Nasdaq, DJIA) have in common with you?

☐ Pays a Mortgage   ☐ Finite Time Horizon
☐ Puts Kids Through School   ☐ Sleeps at Night
☐ None of the Above   ☐ Retires

Three Investment Truths (Correct Perceptions)

1. Expert forecasts are seldom accurate. Your portfolio strategy and investments should not be influenced by their flawed ability to divine the future.

2. Experts will not forecast big moves (black swans, anomalies). There is safety in consensus. An extreme forecast that is incorrect could cost the analyst his job.

3. Diversification is meant to underperform in bull markets. Diversifying is done to spread and reduce risk, thus we ought to expect returns to be lower in bull markets. It is only over complete economic cycles that we experience the real value of diversification.

Key Takeaways

① Our perception, which is fueled by past experience and current beliefs, drives our behavior.

② Perceptions can be wrong and may lead to costly investment decisions.

③ Reflecting on important questions can keep us focused on the correct perceptions.

④ Seek out investment truths—not stereotypes, rumors, or clichés—to develop the correct perception. (This book contains some important investment truths)

My Notes

Chapter Eleven

The Need For
a Written Investment Plan

"If you fail to plan you are planning to fail."

—Benjamin Franklin

Up to now, we have discussed factors that influence us to make poor investment decisions. To review:

1) We are physiologically hardwired to make hasty decisions without much thought.

2) Market volatility can cause us to become emotional and lose our sense of where we are and where we want to go.

3) We like instant feedback (gratification), which influences us to act based on short-term outcomes.

4) The aversion to uncertainty makes us seek some certainty, even if it is just an illusion—such as with market predictions.

5) We tend to micromanage our investments because it makes us *feel* in control.

6) The media often causes us to focus on short-term events and makes it difficult to differentiate important news from noise.

7) We believe we are better at investing than we really are.

8) Our decisions are often influenced by reference points such as our profit/loss on an investment and past performance.

9) We detest loss, and may make unwise decisions in an *attempt* to avoid loss.

10) Our perception can be faulty.

Individually or combined, these points lead investors to make poor decisions that can be very costly.

What do we do? We need to do what we've been told to do for years: Create an investment plan and stick to it. We have heard it over and over, but now we understand why. We need a plan because it will provide the framework to help us overcome our natural tendencies to do the wrong thing at the wrong time.

Developing a Written Plan

I am a big advocate for having a *written* investment plan. The plan will not only help us remember our goals and strategies, but we can also refer to it when times get tough so it can help us stay the course.

An investment plan may also be known as an Investment Policy Statement. These plans detail your needs, goals, and constraints. They provide a framework and map for how you are going to get from where you are today to where you want to be in the future.

Here are a few things you may want to include in your plan. This isn't inclusive, just some of the more important considerations:

1. Identify your financial needs and goals. What are you investing for? What will be your future spending needs? Besides just surviving in retirement, what would you like to do to enrich your life? How much will that cost?

2. Given where you are now, how much do you need to save and what is the required return to achieve your objectives?

3. How much loss are you able and *willing* to tolerate in the short term (risk tolerance)?

   Risk-profiling instruments capture your risk level at a certain point in time. But risk preferences often change based on both personal and external circumstances. In rising markets, people are optimistic about the future, may be influenced by dopamine, and may become more comfortable taking risks. In down markets, fear and anxiety influence investors to reduce their risk preference to preserve what they have. Since risk is not a static measure, it may be helpful to identify your *threshold of pain.*

   This is the point at which your amygdala is likely to activate, and you become sorely tempted to sell. We all have this threshold, whether we identify it or not. Many investors sold near the bottom in 2009, not because they wanted to realize losses but because, unknown to them, they had breached their threshold of pain. Their amygdala was screaming at them to "get to safety." They obeyed their neurological signals at a significant cost.

How much money could you lose before you lost sleep at night?

If you have a $500,000 portfolio, and it dropped to $400,000, would that cause you to lose sleep? What if it went to $300,000? Find the dollar value that would cause you to lose sleep at night, and you will have identified *your* threshold of pain.

The next step is to create a portfolio that will help you achieve your goals while minimizing the probability of breaching that threshold of pain. The portfolio should reflect your objectives while accounting for constraints such as liquidity, time horizon, and how much loss you can tolerate.

I suggest an "all weather" portfolio. Since we don't know whether the next downturn is a great buying opportunity or the first step to much larger losses until well after the fact, it is important that our portfolios be able to perform in both good and bad markets. Chasing the "winning" strategies is a losing proposition. A buy-and-hold portfolio yields much greater returns than a portfolio that tries to time the market.[51]

The ability to hold a portfolio while experiencing losses is difficult. So you may need to have some sort of diversified portfolio to reduce the downside potential. When creating a diversified portfolio, you may want to consider not just stocks and bonds, but also other options that do not move in tandem with stocks and bonds. Since a core goal of a diversified portfolio is to reduce risk, you should not expect it to outperform in bull markets. It is typically only over

---

51 "Quantifying the Impact of Chasing Fund Performance." Retrieved August 7, 2015, at https://institutional.vanguard. com/VGApp/iip/site/institutional/researchcommentary/article/ InvResChasingFundPerf?oeaut=FaJfsFBlHa

an extended period of time that you will see the real value of diversification.

Buy-and-hold strategy superior to performance-chasing strategy

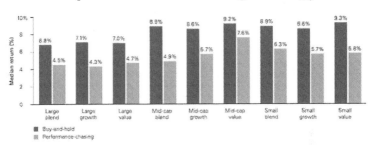

Source: Vanguard

1 Using U.S. equity fund redemption data from the Investment Company Institute for the 15 years from 1998 through 2013, we estimated that the average mutual fund holding period just exceeded three years. Admittedly, redemption ratios are an imperfect measure of mutual fund holding periods, but given a lack of direct evidence on the holding periods of mutual fund investors, we believe this is a reasonable proxy.

2 Although the results are not displayed in this research note, we performed this analysis using a variety of trading rules and time periods and observed similar outcomes.

4. **You may also want to consider a tactical strategy to take advantage of volatility.**

   Creating a series of "if-then" statements that dictate what course of action to take in future market events can be of significant benefit. An example of an if-then statement would be:

   If the market drops 15 percent from its high, then I will

   _____.

   What will you do? Will you do nothing? Review your investment plan? What action will you take? And doing "nothing" is a course of action.

   Let's say the market keeps dropping and is now 25 percent below its high, what will you do? Meet with your financial advisor? Will you think about buying more or be influenced to sell low?

   What if the market drops 35 percent from its high? Perhaps you will move a certain percentage from cash/bonds to stocks … or, in other words, have a systematic process to buy low. These if-then statements can be very effective in creating a future action plan for potential market outcomes.

This strategy can also work on the way up as you identify points where you might want to reduce your exposure to risk, or in other words "sell high." The key here in the plan is to be specific. Most investors have a plan. But it's in their head. Their plan is to "buy low and sell high." The problem is that their plan is too ambiguous; it doesn't define any specific actions.

If the market is down 20 percent from its high, is that low? Not if the market is about to go down 20 percent more. And there is a good chance that is what you are thinking because negative news and market losses fuel each other. A written plan that identifies what is low and what is high will help you know exactly when to take action and what action to take.

This pre-commitment portion of the if-then statement is important. You can choose to invest emotionally or thoughtfully. However, if you don't create an action plan now — when you're thinking logically and making deliberate decisions — then you are delaying the decision until you are influenced by emotions.

Emotional investing feels better, but thoughtful investing is better.

Your Optimal Plan

A customized investment plan based on your preferences will help you make the optimal choices *for you*. As a reminder, an optimization method done by finance experts assumes you don't make any mistakes and your emotions don't influence you. I am all about doing the optimal thing, but the optimal plan for you is the plan you will be able to stick with through thick and thin. Don't be a strategy chaser. Find something that works best for your DNA and stick with it.

Let's be realistic. From time to time, we will make mistakes and deviate from our plan. We will underestimate the intensity of both fear and greed and give into the thinking: "This time is different." And we will make decisions that are contrary to our investment plan. That's okay. We are human. But we need to recognize when we have made an error and promptly return to our target allocation.

How do we do that? No one wants to move a chunk of cash into the market all at once because we know from Murphy's law that the moment we do it, the market will go down. Investors often just wait for the next correction. The problem is we don't know when that will happen. In the meantime, we're not investing optimally for ourselves because we're not following our plan. We're simply market timing. The fear of doing the wrong thing at the wrong time is strong—so strong that we may not be able to overcome it with willpower. We need to do something different to recognize our emotions, and at the same time move toward the target allocation.

Making incremental adjustments may help. If you are 20 percent off from your target allocation, why not move 2 percent per month for 10 months? Yes, you will not get there overnight, but you will get there. And it takes away the emotional risk that keeps investors on the sidelines for months, if not years, waiting for the right time to get back in. The brain prefers things that are black and white; all or none. Sure, we may not be doing it all at once, but at least we are getting back to our plan.

The plan is just the first step, the framework. Now comes the harder part, the discipline.

My Notes

Chapter Twelve

The Value of a Personal Financial Trainer

Assuming you have created a plan, I can assure you that at some point you will be tempted to abandon that plan. When markets are volatile, losses are mounting, and things seem like they can only get worse, it will be very difficult to stick with the plan.

You will rationalize your way right out of the plan. I know exactly what you are going to say to yourself, "Had I known then what I know today, I would have never agreed to this plan." You will need discipline.

The idea that "this time is different" permeates the financial markets during periods of significant expansion or contraction. Many investors focus their time and energy trying to predict the next crisis, the next black swan. They attempt to time their movements in and out of stocks and bonds based on their viewpoints and best intentions. We do not know what will cause the next crisis until it's too late, but the good news is that we don't have to know.

It really doesn't matter what will cause the next crisis. What we know is that in the years ahead the market will experience times of expansion and gains as well as times of contraction and loss. That is the economic and market cycle. So rather than spending energy on that which has no value, let us spend our energy on creating the right investment plan for us, and having the discipline to stick to that plan. We will need our energy to remain disciplined.

The intensity of our emotions is stronger than our good intentions, and is often stronger than our willpower. We may be able to fight off our instincts to chase returns or sell low for a period of time, but the market can be irrational for a long time. Eventually, our willpower will wear down. If I am tempted to eat a piece of chocolate cake, I may be able to abstain for a period. But as time passes and I see that cake (and get more hungry), there will come a point in time when I say, "What the heck, I'm going for it." At that time, I will not only eat one piece but may eat several pieces to satisfy the pent-up demand. Similarly, after experiencing a long period of losses, we may be influenced to not just take a little "off the table," we may sell it all.

Willpower and intention may not be sufficient to overcome the urges. Were they sufficient in the past? If you do the same thing, expect the same result, regardless of intentions. The definition of insanity is doing the same thing over and over and expecting different results. We need to do something different.

We need to engage a personal financial trainer.

The Personal Financial Trainer

The role of a personal trainer that you find at the gym is to put together a fitness plan that takes into account your goals and your physical condition. They teach you how to lift weights and exercise properly, and encourage you to keep at it when your muscles and stamina are near their end. They help you stay disciplined to your plan so you can reach your goals.

A personal financial trainer also puts together a plan that is right for you based on your goals as well as your financial and emotional condition. A personal financial trainer should teach you investment truths and important principles to successful investing. They help you learn to filter the noise of the media and deal with market volatility. And when things get tough, they are there to encourage you to keep at it. They are there to help you stay disciplined to your plan so you can reach your goals.

Imagine you have a son entering high school trying out for the football team. In preparation, he wants to increase his strength with a weight-lifting program. So you drop him off at the local gym. He has never lifted weights before. What would you tell him? Would you say, "Just watch what others are doing and do that"? You've seen people at the gym. Your son would get hurt. Instead, you would either show him how to do it yourself, or hire a personal trainer to teach your son how to work out safely and effectively. That should be our approach with investing.

Most investors get their advice from the media and take their cues from what others are doing. "This security just went up. Everybody else is buying it. Analysts say it will go higher. It is probably a good idea to get some of it myself." A lot of times, without knowing it, we are either following the media's recommendation or following the herd. Neither knows who we are, what our goals are, or what would be best for us. Doesn't sound like a sound strategy.

A better strategy would be to engage a financial advisor who will act as our personal financial trainer. We should select an advisor who is not interested in selling a product, but rather in creating a plan that is right for us—and providing the discipline we need to stick with it.

The Right Advisor

I am an advocate for independent, knowledgeable financial professionals who can think on their own and who put the investment *process* above investment *products* and clairvoyance. They put you and your needs above all else. Their ability to put you first does not have to do with the firm they work for; it is about the mental independence of the financial advisor. Advisors at large brokerage firms or small independent shops can either have your best interest at heart or their own interest.

It's about the advisor's personality and philosophy, the way they conduct business. This is about finding the right individual *for you.*

When I mention that you need a knowledgeable financial professional, the knowledge I'm referring to is whether advisors recognize the psychological factors that influence their own decisions, as well as what influences investor decisions. It has been found that economic behavior is 70 percent psychological and 30 percent rational.[52] Most financial professionals are trained on the rational level, dealing with market data and economic figures. Are the advisors that you interview aware of the psychological influences?

Since psychological factors influence the majority of our financial decisions, if advisors don't understand what influences various investor decisions, then they are not going to be of great help. Make sure that the advisor you select understands how behavior and emotion influence investor decisions. That's the only way they will be able to give you the best advice and make sure you are getting your money's worth. Advisors that "get" the be-

---

52   de Bono, Edward. *I Am Right -You Are Wrong.* ©1991. Penguin Books. New York.

havioral aspect of investing are much more valuable than those who don't.

Vanguard recently broke down the value of a good, qualified financial advisor. Their analysis shows that an advisor's value can add more than 2 percent per year to return. And you know what the biggest factor is in the added value? Behavioral coaching. According to Vanguard, behavioral coaching adds 1.50 percent per year.[53] In other words, it is expected that you will earn 1.5 percent more per year by engaging an advisor that "gets" the psychology of investing than if you had not.

Most financial advisors offer some sort of investment and/or financial planning. They help identify your risk and recommend portfolios of securities commensurate with that risk. There is some value there. But the biggest value is in the behavioral coaching. So if your advisor is charging a 1 percent advisory fee, the behavioral coaching alone pays for it. Add in financial planning and other services, and you are getting a pretty good deal.

Asking the Right Questions

When you are searching for the right advisor, there are some questions you should ask to be sure they are qualified. Finding out the advisor's experience, investment philosophy, fees, and potential conflicts of interest are important.

But don't forget to ask questions such as these to see whether the advisor "gets it" on a behavioral level:

53 Kinniry, Francis M., Jaconetti, Colleen M., DiJoseph, Michael A., Zilbering, Yan. "Putting a value on your value." March 2014. Retrieved August 7, 2015, at http://www.vanguard.com/pdf/ISGQVAA.pdf

1) How are you going to ensure that emotions don't get in your way when you are advising me?

A response that refers to an investment plan or process is desirable.

2) What did you do to help clients who wanted to sell during a time of market losses, such as in 2008-2009 or the Ebola outbreak in 2014?

Telling them not to sell is not a sufficient answer. Seek examples of how an advisor may have empathized with the feelings of the investors and coached them to stay the course.

3) What do you do or what would you recommend I do if I end up making a bad investment decision? What if I am uncomfortable getting back in?

A systematic investment plan will eliminate the temptation to time the market and get you to your desired allocation.

4) What is your investment process, and does that process change based upon market conditions?

A process does not mean you never make a change—it's simply the big picture, and may include tactical adjustments. The process may change based upon personal circumstances, but should not change based on market outcomes alone.

5) What role does psychology play in investing?

This important, open-ended question will tell you right away whether the advisor has any training in this area. An advisor who can discuss some of the concepts in this book "gets it."

Providing Objective Advice

These financial professionals are subject to the same influences that all of us are.

We're all human. But because they are not managing their money but yours, they are able to remain more objective and allow reason, thought, and logic to drive their advice. When we are providing advice on an issue someone else has, it is much easier for us to provide rational and non-emotional advice.

Let's say you have a friend who comes to you for advice in a difficult situation. Your friend is highly emotional, and you give him sound advice. But it's advice that you may not follow when you are in the same situation. We all do that: Do as I say, not as I do. It's not because we're hypocrites. It's because of the emotional pull. Saying it is one thing—doing it is completely different.

Advisors can remain objective because it's not their money, and good advisors are trained to remain disciplined.

A good advisor can help you design the right plan and provide the discipline to stick with the plan. A good financial advisor becomes your coach, your advocate, and your greatest cheerleader when times are difficult. They are pulling for you to reach *your* goals.

Good advisors are not concerned about getting you to invest in a certain way, or about what others in your situation may be doing. They focus on doing what's best for you. A good advisor will help customize a plan that is right for *you*, and provide the discipline to help you stick to it.

My Notes

Chapter Thirteen

Wrapping it Up

It doesn't matter how much you know, it matters what you do with what you know.

We are all hardwired to think certain ways and have neurological responses that help us in everyday life. This is crucial for our survival and ability to live in a complex world. But when it comes to making financial decisions, these same things can influence us to make costly decisions.

There has been much research done by Dalbar, Inc. on the costs of emotional investing. But they are not unique. While Dalbar, Inc. has found that stock and bond investors underperform their index, Morningstar® has found that investors underperform the very mutual funds they are invested in. How is that even possible? Both firms come to the same conclusion: it is the timing of purchases and sales by investors. We like to buy after we have seen evidence of gains and sell after we have experienced losses.

It sounds so simple, "Buy low and sell high." Yet it is one of the most difficult things we can do as investors. If you have found yourself making some of these same mistakes—being influenced by experts, the media, and your emotions to make poor decisions—all I can say is welcome to the human race. You are not alone. I am passionate about these things because I recognize how they have influenced me to make poor decisions. I am still influenced by them, but I am doing something about it.

Wisdom is the application of knowledge. It doesn't matter how much you know, it matters what you do with what you know. Now you know. The question is: will you do something about it?

I list below a few applicable techniques that will help you take a more thoughtful and deliberate approach to your investment decisions, despite the urges to do otherwise.

Control the Controllable

We need to first recognize what part of investing is in our control and what part we have no control over. Unfortunately, we can't control volatility, public policy, or market returns. But we can control our investment plan and our reaction to market events. Let's use our energy more productively by focusing our efforts on those things we can control.

Practice Strategic Procrastination

When you are tempted to act impulsively, the best thing to do is delay the response. Commit to delay a specific period of time before each investment decision, to allow time for the impulse to wear out, and for thinking brain to engage. During that delay, be sure to reflect on the situation … pondering both the possibility of good outcomes and how you could be wrong.

Make Volatility Your Friend

Fear of market volatility is primarily a mindset and the result of focusing too much on short-term outcomes. If you have several years before you plan to liquidate your investment portfolio, volatility has a tremendous potential to be your friend. But that is your choice. You can choose to fear lower security prices, or view them as an opportunity to enhance long-term gains.

Ignore the Forecasts

Forecasts feed our innate desire for certainty. Yet, the accuracy of a given forecast is far from certain. But because our brain desires some sense of certainty it may subconsciously be influenced to act based on a specific forecast, especially if the person is deemed an "expert." Analysts and economists are great at crunching numbers and writing reports. They are awful at forecasting. That's not their fault—the market is unpredictable by nature. Their fault is pretending they can accurately predict the market. But we tune into it, so they do it.

Filter the Noise

The financial media's job is to get you to tune in. They have a lot of programming space to fill (be it TV, newspaper, radio, or internet). If it's a big news day, that is an easy task. Most days are not big news days, but they still need to get you to tune in. So they fill the time with speculation about the future, with experts who pretend they know what is going to happen, and with stories that are newsworthy only because there is no other news. The media influences short-term thinking so you will tune in tomorrow. A friend of mine once said, "If you hang around the barbershop long enough, you're going to get a haircut." Indeed, if we listen long enough, we may be influenced to act on the noise.

Enhance Your Investing Skill

Because markets are unpredictable and random over the short term, skill in investing is not about selecting the right security. It's not about timing the market top or bottom. Real skill in investing is about having the patience and discipline to stick with your investment plan, even when it isn't working. It didn't take any skill whatsoever to buy a tech stock in 1999, but it took a tremendous amount of skill for Warren Buffett to not invest in technology because he didn't understand how the companies would make money and survive. He "underperformed" for quite some time while tech stocks took off. But he stuck to his guns, which ended up being hugely profitable … only after he had the patience and discipline to wait it out several years.

Define Your Threshold of Pain

Risk profiles such as "conservative" or "aggressive" are ambiguous. What exactly does that mean? What loss is acceptable? It is important, as part of defining your risk profile, to identify how much loss (in dollars) you are able and willing to accept. One of the benefits of experiencing two significant market downturns in the past 15 years is the ability to quantify how a future bear market may affect your portfolio. If your portfolio, as it is today, could lose more money than your threshold, then you may want to revisit how much risk is in the portfolio.

Seek Out Investment Truths

There are a lot of people who want to give you advice. Much of that advice will be based on personal experience, past markets, gut feelings, statistical inference, quantitative analysis, etc. But one thing we have learned through the history of the stock market (and detailed in this book) is that each of those have failed at some point in time. An investment truth is always true; it is not dependent on certain factors or assumptions. One investment truth is that markets go up and down. As you seek and learn investment truths, the next step is to adhere to principles that support those truths. One example of an investment principle for the market's volatility is rebalancing—a systematic way to purchase securities low and sell them high.

Get a Written Plan

"I got my plan. It's in my head. I'm going to buy low and sell high." Many an investor has said this. Most investors do this. We have good intentions, but don't take the time to construct a written, detailed plan to ensure we realize our intentions. A plan not only specifies your purpose for investing, but also provides a roadmap to help you get to your goals. It is something that can be referred to and updated as personal conditions change. Whether you create your plan by yourself or engage a trusted advisor, it is an essential element to help you overcome the automatic, biological impulses that influence poor investment decisions.

Be Disciplined. Be Disciplined.

Okay. I said it twice. That is because no matter how good your intentions are, even if you have a written investment plan, you will be tempted to abandon your plan. We may remember how great we felt in 1999 and how horrible we felt in 2008-2009. But we likely have forgotten the intensity of those feelings—greed and fear. I strongly encourage you to engage a trusted third party—a Personal Financial Trainer—to help you stay disciplined and to encourage you to stay with the plan you created. This can be a financial advisor, family member, or friend. Whoever you choose, I suggest that they have an understanding of your goals, risk, how the investment markets work, and the psychological influences on decision-making.

Final Comments

This book has been a labor of love. I love talking about the behavioral concepts in this book and teaching them to both financial advisors and retail investors. I get hired regularly by the financial industry to do in-person presentations, which is a lot of fun. I have met so many wonderful people over the years. I have heard so many stories. Everything I write about in this book is ordinary and commonplace. We generally don't discuss our mistakes, but I can assure you these are very common mistakes. I personally have made most (if not every single one) of them.

The good news is we own our future. While we may not be able to control what happens to us, we can control how we respond. I hope this book has provided you with some ideas, a framework, and a hope that tomorrow is the start of better investment decisions.

JAY

If you would like additional resources, please check out my website. I have provided many resources including blogs, e-learning training videos, published articles, and my graduate thesis that started it all: *The Irrational Investor's Risk Profile.*

www.theEmotionalinvestor.org

***Exclusively for readers of this book, you can obtain a copy of an article I wrote for financial advisors (that pertains to all investors) titled: "Break that Habit: How to Help Clients Develop Better Investment Habits." It discusses how habits are created, and how to replace a bad habit with a good one. The article focuses on investments, but the techniques can be applied to all aspects of life. Go to www.theEmotionalinvestor.org/habit or scan the QR code below.

If you have found this book to be of value, please share it with another. These behavioral influences affect everyone and every demographic. Behavioral biases are no respecter of persons.

About the Author

Jay Mooreland is founder of The Emotional Investor. He is a Certified Financial Planner Professional, behavioral economist, speaker, and educator on investor behavior. He has also authored several articles published in industry journals on the topic of investor behavior. He helps financial professionals and individual investors understand how behavioral biases influence our choices, and what we can do to improve our decision-making process.

Jay travels the world speaking at conferences on the topic of investor behavior. His interactive presentations focus on the application of behavioral theory. Additionally, Jay has created several tools that financial professionals can implement, such as *Understanding My Client, The 9 Habits of Successful Investors* and *Personality Driven Financial Consulting.* These tools provide a framework for financial professionals to help investors make less emotional, more thoughtful decisions.

Jay has a Bachelor of Science in Business Finance from San Jose State University and a Master of Science in Applied Economics from the University of Minnesota, where he authored the academic study The Irrational Investor's Risk Profile. In his spare time, Jay enjoys cycling, running and traveling. Jay, his wife and two children live in Saint Paul, MN.

For more information, please visit

www.theEmotionalinvestor.org

92612256R00078

Made in the USA
Columbia, SC
30 March 2018